Chairmaking Simplified

KERRY PIERCE

POPULAR WOODWORKING BOOKS
CINCINNATI, OHIO
www.popularwoodworking.com

Read This Important Safety Notice

To prevent accidents, keep safety in mind while you work. Use the safety guards installed on power equipment; they are for your protection. When working on power equipment, keep fingers away from saw blades, wear safety goggles to prevent injuries from flying wood chips and sawdust, wear hearing protection and consider installing a dust vacuum to reduce the amount of airborne sawdust in your woodshop. Don't wear loose clothing, such as neckties or shirts with loose sleeves, or jewelry, such as rings, necklaces or bracelets, when working on power equipment. Tie back long hair to prevent it from getting caught in your equipment. People who are sensitive to certain chemicals should check the chemical content of any product before using it. The authors and editors who compiled this book have tried to make the contents as accurate and correct as possible. Plans, illustrations, photographs and text have been carefully checked. All instructions, plans and projects should be carefully read, studied and understood before beginning construction. Due to the variability of local conditions, construction materials, skill levels, etc., neither the author nor Popular Woodworking Books assumes any responsibility for any accidents, injuries, damages or other losses incurred resulting from the material presented in this book. Prices listed for supplies and equipment were current at the time of publication and are subject to change.

Metric Conversion Chart

to convert	to	multiply by
Inches	Centimeters	2.54
Centimeters	Inches	0.4
Feet	Centimeters	30.5
Centimeters	Feet	0.03
Yards	Meters	0.9
Meters	Yards	1.1

Distributed in Canada by Fraser Direct
100 Armstrong Avenue
Georgetown, Ontario L7G 5S4
Canada

Distributed in the U.K. and Europe by David & Charles
Brunel House
Newton Abbot
Devon TQ12 4PU
England
Tel: (+44) 1626 323200
Fax: (+44) 1626 323319
E-mail: postmaster@davidandcharles.co.uk

Distributed in Australia by Capricorn Link
P.O. Box 704
Windsor, NSW 2756
Australia

Visit our Web site at www.popularwoodworking.com or our consumer Web site at www.fwbookstore.com for information on more resources for woodworkers and other arts and crafts projects.

Other fine Popular Woodworking Books are available from your local bookstore or direct from the publisher.

12   11   10   09   08   5   4   3   2   1

Library of Congress Cataloging-in-Publication Data

Pierce, Kerry.
   Chairmaking simplified / by Kerry Pierce.-- 1st ed.
      p. cm.
   ISBN-13: 978-1-55870-827-3 (pbk. : alk. paper)
   ISBN-10: 1-55870-827-8 (pbk. : alk. paper)
   1. Chairs. 2. Woodwork. I. Title.
   TS880.P525 2008
   684.1'3--dc22

                                   2007051181

Acquisitions Editor: David Thiel
Senior Editor: Jim Stack
Designer: Brian Roeth
Production Coordinator: Mark Griffin
Photographer: Lindsey Beckwith
Illustrator: Kevin Pierce

About the Author

After earning a bachelor's degree in English from Bowling Green State University, and a master's degree in art from

Ohio University, Kerry Pierce began a 30-year career as a professional furniture maker. He has specialized in Shaker and Shaker-inspired work for much of that career. Many of his 13 books and 80 magazine articles focus on Shaker woodworking. He has shown his Shaker-inspired work in a number of regional venues, most recently at "Ohio Furniture by Contemporary Masters" at the Decorative Arts Center of Ohio. He has served as Contributing Editor of *Woodwork* magazine since 1995, and is also a regular instructor at the Marc Adams School in Indianapolis, teaching most often about Shaker-style chair-making.

Dedication

For Sally, who taught me to read and to love books; for Jim, who taught me the pleasures of craftsmanship; for Elaine, Emily, and Andy, who have made my life complete; and for all the good people at Popular Woodworking Books, in particular Jim Stack and David Thiel.

And a special thanks to Sarah and the Larks.

I also want to acknowledge the assistance of the Warren County Historical Museum (wchmuseum.com) in Lebanon, Ohio, for allowing us access to their excellent Shaker furniture collection.

(The Mark Soukop profile ran originally in *Woodwork* magazine, and the Mike Herrel profile originally ran in *Woodshop News*.)

Preface

Let's face it, chairmaking can be intimidating. It's not really like any other branch of the woodworking tree. Who but a chair-maker knows how to use an inshave, an adze, or a side-rung-mortise jig? In fact, who but a chairmaker knows what these tools are? In addition, chair-making requires a working knowledge of technologies and skills foreign to most woodworkers. Who but a chairmaker regularly steams and bends wooden parts? Who but a chairmaker knows how to weave a seat from splint or Shaker tape or cattail leaves? In fact, who but a chairmaker knows cattail leaves are useful for anything at all?

Chairmaking can be intimidating, but it doesn't have to be, and that's what this book is all about. Its mission is to present simple and straightforward approaches to the chair-making craft, to make it possible for any woodworker with moderate skills to find success.

You will find more step-by-step photos here than in any other book on the subject. You will find clear, carefully-rendered measured drawings of a wider range of chairs than has ever before appeared in a single book — from post-and-rung to Windsor, from Arts & Crafts to Appalachian country.

More important, in keeping with book's mission to simplify the chairmaking process, you will find on these pages jigs and fixtures that have never before appeared in any book. After almost 30 years as a chairmaker, a chairmaking instructor, and the author of three books and dozens of magazine articles on the subject of chairmaking, I decided to rethink the jig landscape, from the ground up, stripping it down so that you won't spend 40 hours building jigs to construct a chair that takes only 20 hours to build.

These methods and jigs are the result not only of my own experiences as a chairmaker; they are also the result of my years as a chairmaking instructor at the Marc Adams School, during which I was able to take a close look at the kinds of questions and problems that surfaced as the students in my classes built their first chairs.

In addition, Michael Herrel, a craftsman from Bexley, Ohio, shares his simplified method for Windsor chairmaking that includes some of the most ingenious shop-made chairmaking methods I've ever seen.

There are few workshop experiences as gratifying as building a chair. If you've ever wanted to try it but felt intimidated by what you've heard, turn the page. Step inside. I think you might find what you're looking for.

Table of Contents

The Genesis Chair

The field of chairmaking is enormous, far too vast to be usefully encompassed in a single volume. It's a craft that includes the simple rock or log positioned near the fire, as well as the bronze Throne of St. Peter in St. Peter's Basilica in the Vatican. It includes every object modified by human hand to provide the human body with a place to sit, even if that modification consists of nothing more complicated than changing the position of a stone so that its flattest surface is on top. It includes those gold-covered and jewel-encrusted thrones on which many craftsmen labored for weeks in order to provide the monarchs of human history with seating places commensurate with their worldly power. But mostly, it consists of those constructions in between these extremes, constructions which have provided you and me, our grandparents and their grandparents with comfortable places on which to

This chair is representative of the thousands made in rural America during the 17th, 18th, and 19th centuries. The seat is woven from hickory bark, and the posts, rungs and slats are made from one or more of those species favored by rural American chair-makers: oak, ash, hickory, or maple — although in its current weathered state, it's difficult to find clues that would make it possible to identify which species was used where.

sit while eating or talking or simply reflecting on the human condition.

This book looks at those in-between chairs, specifically the three types that have dominated European and American chairmaking in the last three hundred years: Windsor-style chairs, post-and-rung chairs and the simple bench.

The Genesis Chair

Early in the summer of 2007, my wife Elaine and I stopped at an antique mall in Florence, Kentucky. We spent less than an hour in the mall and, remarkably, Elaine found nothing to buy, but I was more fortunate. I found something I had been seeking for almost three years.

In the 15-20 antique malls Elaine and I had visited in Ohio and Pennsylvania during those three years, I had seen dozens of country chairs of the same general configuration as the example I found in Florence, Kentucky. Each of these Ohio and Pennsylvania specimens had four posts into which approximately-round rungs had been mortised, and each had a seat woven around the top row of rungs. But all the chairs I had examined before our arrival at the mall in Florence, Kentucky, featured work that had been accomplished with the aid of a machine, even if that machine was a simple spring-pole lathe. What I had been looking for was a chair in which every single element had been wrest-ed from a tree using only hand tools: a froe, a club, a handsaw, a drawknife and other similarly simple tools.

The Florence chair is not an exem-plary model of craftsmanship. Its parts are crudely fashioned and crudely assembled. The maker invested little effort in regularizing the drawknifed facets which compose the outside diameters of the posts and rungs. The slat mortises are oversized with gaps showing all around each end of each slat, and while some of the gaps can

The chair frame is assem-bled by placing round rung tenons into round mortises drilled into the posts. Notice that the rungs and posts were not lathe-turned. They were, instead, broken out of the log, split and shaved to size. Notice also the lack of a shoulder adjacent to the rung tenon. Such chair-making niceties would have required more time and perhaps more skill than the maker had available.

The slats were broken out and shaved to thickness. Notice that this slat was shaved to follow the natural undulations of the wood from which it is made. This practice produces a slat with continuous grain which makes the slat resistant to cross-grain fracture.

The seat is woven in a sim-ple pattern from the inner bark of the hickory tree, an uncommonly strong seating material, but it is time and effort-consuming to harvest. Notice the joint on the top surface of the seat just ahead of the back left post. These joints were usually made on the bottom side of the woven seat to keep them out of view.

The hickory bark runs around the post so that the strand being used to form the warp (the strands run-ning from the front to the back rails) can be used to start the weave (the strands running from side to side).

This pair of Brewster chairs is typical of the Pilgrim post-and-rung style that informed much rural American chairmaking in the two centuries following the Pilgrims' arrival in America. I sold these two chairs, unseated and unfinished, 20 years ago to a husband-and-wife team of collectors who took them to another craftsman for the application of a distressed finish. The turnings were beaten with flat boards and chains. A rasp was used to create wear. The chairs were then covered with a heavy, inky-black finish before they were taken to another craftsman to be seated in rush.

be attributed to slat shrinkage, most are the result of sloppy workmanship. The hickory-bark seat has joints on both the top and bottom surfaces. These are joints a more dedicated craftsman would have kept hidden on the bottom of the seat. In fact, I doubt that in the antique marketplace the chair is worth any more than the $50 I paid for it.

But if you set aside the issues of craftsmanship and aesthetics, the Florence chair has a brutish elegance that is completely faithful to the tradi-

tion of chairmaking as it was practiced in the culture that produced it. It was built by hand, using good wood-to-wood joinery, without the aide of any metal fasteners. It was almost certainly made from locally available materials that likely could have been found within a few steps of the home of the craftsman who made it.

But the Florence chair is valuable to me because it represents the form from which all other American post-and-rung chairs are descended. It is a representative example of the tens of thousands of chairs built in backwoods communities in New England, in the Appalachian states and even in the South.

These were chairs made to provide people with places to sit while they sat in their bedrooms to remove their shoes, while they read at the kitchen table in the light of a coal oil lamp, while they sat on the front porches of their homes and watched the pas-

sage of the seasons. These were chairs made by and for people who lacked the resources to purchase finer examples built by more accomplished craftsmen working in well-equipped shops.

It is a form that originated in the Pilgrim's post-and-rung chairs built in New England in the early 17th century, which itself originated in the earlier forms produced in Elizabethan England.

The reproduction Brewster chairs, shown at left, are typical of those Pilgrim examples. In manner of construction, the Genesis chair is much like the Brewster chair. Both styles feature round-rung tenons housed in round mortises drilled into round posts. Both styles feature seats woven around four rungs.

Despite the fundamental similarities in construction, the articulation of the parts comprising the two different styles are different. The Pilgrim chairs are made up of lathe-turned parts of

The term *chairmaking* denotes a loose confederation of crafts, among them seat weaving. Leonard Seaton, a 64-year old Londoner, sits on a city curb as he repairs a cane chair seat in 1951. He learned the craft at age 12 after leaving school. For the next 52 years, he practiced the trade, offering customers the convenience of house-to-house service.

a complexity that requires an experienced workman with a knowledge of the Elizabethan chairmaking tradition.

The spring-pole lathes on which the parts for Pilgrim chairs were originally turned are not complex machines, but they are more complex than most tools in the woodworking arsenal of craftsmen in 17th-, 18th- and early 19th-century rural America. Rural chairmakers of the period were often not professionals. They typically built chairs in the evening after spending the day farming, hunting or working at some other pioneer trade. While their tool kits usually included a few woodworking tools and perhaps a few smithing tools, they had little need for something a complex as a lathe. When they built chairs, they did so using the simple tools already at their disposal, building theirs to resemble other examples they had seen. Those examples might have included a Pilgrim original, but more likely those examples were several generations away from the Pilgrim examples.

Despite their lack of access to sophisticated tooling, chairmakers working in rural America have produced four-centuries worth of eminently functional seating furniture.

In the 20th and 21st centuries, Americans have demonstrated an affection for hand-built chairs. This uncomfortable love seat is obviously handmade, using, as its frame, limbs and twigs from which the bark has been removed. A seat was then woven around the top set of rungs.

For over 100 years, the field of chairmaking has been dominated by factories which have turned out low-cost chairs by the tens of thousands. The bow-back Windsor in which the young man on the left is sitting in this late 1940s photo is one such chair. The wicker chair on the right in which the older man sits and smokes a pipe is likely an English import.

1

Organizing the Chair-making Process

The method of chair-making I demonstrate in this book is the result of several decades of study, thinking and experimentation. Those decades are marked by chairmaking failures, as well as, thankfully, chairmaking successes. The method I present here isn't the only successful method for the construction of post-and-rung chairs, and I would never contend that it's the best method, but it is an exhaustively tested method that routinely produces successful chairs in the shops of individual chairmakers working in small shops without expensive equipment.

And this method has been tested in shops other than my own. I've taught my method to dozens of craftsmen at the Marc Adams School of Woodworking in Indianapolis, and many of those students have gone home to their shops and put my method to work producing, in some cases, dozens of chairs.

As you'll see on the pages of this book, my power tools are relatively

Herb Pfundt, who made the chair in this picture, never took my class. He learned to build chairs from reading a couple of my earlier books on the subject. In fact, he learned well enough to become a valuable assistant at several of my classes at the Marc Adams School.

low-end consumer-grade tools, the kinds of tools you can buy at Sears, Lowe's or Home Depot. Some are used tools I picked up at flea markets or antique malls. I didn't purchase inexpensive tools in order to make a philosophic point about the potential of these tools. I bought them because they were all I could afford as my wife and I struggled to support a family on my salary as a public school teacher.

I would have paid $2000 for a lathe with more space between centers and hefty cast-iron components, but I didn't have the two grand. It was hard enough to come up with the $200 for my Sears lathe.

I mention this because, at least in part as a result of the limitations of my low-end tools, my method has to proceed in an orderly manner with Step No.3 following Step No.2, which follows Step No.1. My method, for example, requires you to drill your

Several years ago Dave Duey took my Shaker rocking chair class at the Marc Adams School in Indianapolis. He was so successful with the chair he made in class that he has since made others using the methods he learned there. He recently sent me an email to which this photo was attached: "Thanks for teaching me," he said in his e-mail. "I just love to make these, and I guess that is what it is all about."

Tim Arnold also took my rocking chair class at the Marc Adams School. During his one week there, he built the rocker, the jigs the rocker requires and a stool as well. He then went home and built more chairs using the methods he'd learned in class. "I just wanted to say how excellent your class was this summer. I enjoyed it so much. I finally got around to making another rocker. This one is larger than the one I made in class. Attached you will see a photo with the class rocker on the right and the new larger one on the left."

Construction Sequence

1. Rip out back posts.
2. Turn back posts, leaving finial elements oversized.
3. Sand back posts.
4. Mark back posts.
5. Finish turning back-post finials and cut off surplus length on the head-stock end of post. (There's more on this subject in the turning chapter.)
6. Cut out slats on the band saw.
7. Finish edges of slats with spokeshave, rasp and sandpaper.
8. Drill back-rung mortises on the front-rung-mortise jig (FRMJ).
9. Bend back posts and slats.
10. Turn and sand rungs and front posts.
11. Mark front posts.
12. Cut out and clean up sawn edges on rockers and arms. If necessary, sculpt edges of arms.
13. Drill front-rung mortises on the FRMJ.
14. Assemble front ladder.
15. After steamed and bent parts have been in the forms for a minimum of one week, remove them from the forms.
16. Chop slat mortises in back posts. Fit each slat into each of its mortises.
17. Assemble back ladder.
18. Drill side-rung mortises on the side-rung-mortise jig (SRMJ) in both the front and back ladders.
19. Shape and fit arms.
20. Install arms.
21. Cut notches for rockers and install rockers.
22. Sand with 150-grit sandpaper if chair is to be painted, with 150, 220 and 320 grits if chair is to be given a natural finish.
23. Apply finish.

back rung mortises before you bend the back posts. If you bend the posts before attempting to drill the back rung mortises, you'll find that the back posts won't fit properly on my FRMJ (front-[and back]-rung-mortise jig). You can still drill those back-rung mortises, but you'll have to employ a different mortising method than the one I explain here. A more expensive, and therefore more versatile, mortising machine would make it possible to alter the step-by-step sequence I've established, but if you're going to use my method you have to follow the steps I've outlined in the order I list them.

The list includes all the steps necessary for an armed rocker, the most complicated chair. Obviously, if you're building a side chair, you can eliminate those references to arms and rockers.

Note: If you're a first-time chair-maker, you might want to copy this

Herb Pfundt also made the chair shown here, without the benefit of formal instruction.

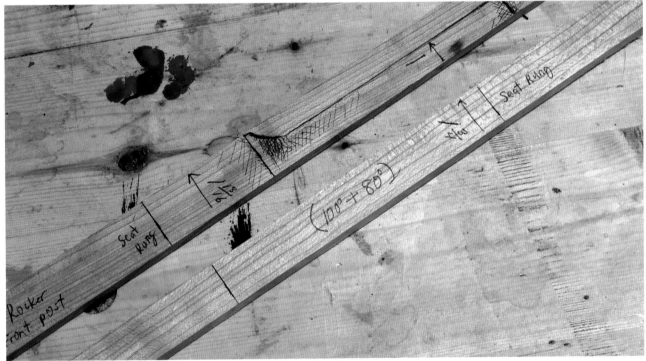

These chair post story sticks for the Union Village rocker illustrate the information that must be recorded on the sticks. The stick at the bottom represents the back post and the stick at the top represents the front post. (I should mention that the post diameters recorded here are the diameters of the original chair, and I changed those diameters on the example I made in order to achieve what I hope is a more satisfying composition.) The contours of the vase under the arm is sketched on the stick so that I can work without keeping a photo on my lathe table. The lines squared across the sticks represent the centers of the various rung locations. The measurements adjacent to the lines with arrowheads indicate post's diameters at those locations.

13

Each of the four sticks at the bottom indicate a different rung. The tenons are located at the shaded sections on the ends of each rung stick. The plywood rocker and arm patterns are next. I made them by attaching paper patterns, on which I'd sketched their shapes, to the plywood pattern stock using rubber cement. I then bandsawed the lines I'd drawn on the paper. The slat pattern is shown at the top of the photo. Notice that additional information is recorded on each of these cutting patterns. On the rocker pattern, I've indicated the placement of the rocker within the ends of the posts, as well as the depth of the notches into which the rockers will be fastened. The arm pattern indicates the position of the through-tenon at the top of the front post. The information sketched on the slat pattern includes the length of each of the chair's four slats, as well as the lengths of each tenon on each end of each slat. (See photo below.) The post sticks are between the slat and arm patterns.

I keep each set of story sticks together with metal clothes hangers I've modified for this purpose. Each of these five clutches of story sticks represents a different chair.

list and put it up somewhere in your shop, because, if work is performed out of sequence, it can create headaches later as you work your way to the finish line.

Story Sticks

Every chair I build is represented by a clutch of story sticks on which I've recorded all the information the construction of that chair requires. There are three kinds of sticks in each clutch. The first includes patterns representing each of the slats, rockers and arms that will be cut on the band saw. The second represents the rungs. In the case of most Shaker-style chairs, the rungs are tapered turnings with a tenon on each end. The story stick indicates the locations and lengths of those tenons, as well

as numbers indicating the diameters of those rungs at various places along their lengths. Some rungs, however, have coves and/or beads, and the locations and contours of those shapes are indicated on the rung sticks. The third includes sticks representing the chair posts. These are more complicated sticks to prepare because there is so much information that needs to be represented on them. To begin with, the posts are typically decorated with turned work, in particular the finials at the top of each back post. Plus, the locations of each rung mortise must be marked on the post sticks. On the back-post sticks, I mark the centers of back-rung mortise locations, as well as slat locations, on one side. Then, on the other side of the stick, I mark the centers of side-

rung and arm mortise locations. On the front-post sticks, I mark the centers of front-rung mortise locations on one side and the centers of side-rung mortises on the other side. Finally, the diameters of the posts at various locations along their lengths need to be identified.

It is possible to make chairs without first preparing story sticks, but there are so many elements on each part of each chair that must be correctly shaped and/or correctly located that the time spent making story sticks is returned to you many times over as you proceed through the chairmaking process.

2

Material Selection

Several years ago, the editors of *Australian Wood Review* sent me a supply of Australian black-wood from which I was to construct a New Lebanon No.6 slat-back side chair, which appears in this book on page 116. The editors sent me one piece of figured blackwood from which I made the slats. The rest was unfigured material.

They wanted me to combine an American form — a Shaker chair — with an Australian material, and I love the chair that resulted from that unlikely combination. But, it is not a chair capable of withstanding much abuse. It's very light — you can lift the entire chair with a single finger — and lightness of weight often translates into material with little resistance to cross-grain fracture. More important, the test rung I turned with a bit of extra blackwood was relatively easy to break, whereas a rung turned from hard maple or ash is all but indestructible.

Fortunately, the design of a Shaker chair seat, with the weight of the sitter spread out along a large number of warp and weave strands of seating material, doesn't

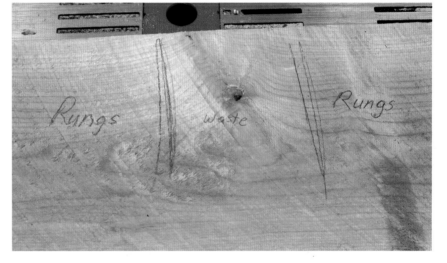

I start work on the posts by cutting the turning-blank board to length. Here I'm deciding where to make my crosscut in 2"-thick maple. I want enough extra length to escape the checking you almost always find on the dried end of a plank, but I don't want so much extra length that I end up wasting material. Typically, I'll add on as much extra length as I can without jeopardizing my chances to get more post-turning blanks from the rest of the board.

require an enormous amount of wood strength in order to provide usefulness, but this particular chair, made from this particular material, doesn't have the degree of redundant strength I like to have in a chair I sell to a customer. Neither does American cherry, although I have sold a number of chairs using that material. Soft maple is also too weak for chairmaking. Of course, all figured material is inherently more fragile than its straight-grained counterpart. Walnut, despite my enormous affection for the way it works, looks, smells and feels offers barely acceptable strength. If you're looking to build a chair that can't be broken no matter how intense the abuse, you should stick with the classic American chairmaking woods: hard maple, white oak, ash and hickory. A carefully built chair with parts fabricated from one of these species is as close to indestructible as anything that will ever leave your shop.

Material Evaluation

A craftsman is engaged with his or her material from the moment it's selected in a lumber yard to the moment the final coat of wax is buffed out prior to

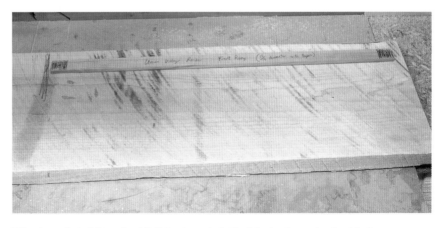

I'll make my crosscuts for rung-blank stock approximately where the scribbled lines are in order to excise this knot. I'll cut the blanks with enough extra length to avoid the grain runout you see on the left side of the knot.

This piece of straight-grained 5/4 hard maple is ideal for front-rung turning blanks.

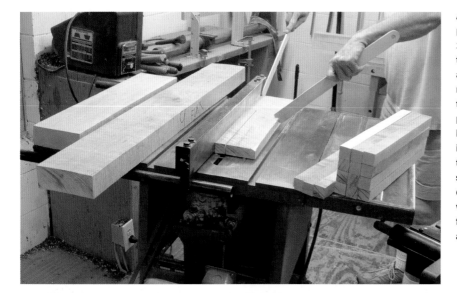

After crosscutting the rough stock to approximate length, I'll rip the rung blanks into 1¹/₄" × 1¹/₄" turning blanks. Notice that the push sticks allow me to keep my fingers away from the action. Notice, too, that I'm not standing in the line of fire directly behind the blade where I might be injured by a piece of kicked-back stock. My table saw has been in this location for 20 years, and twice in that period, rung turning blanks have been thrown through the window behind my table saw. One sailed almost twenty feet down my driveway — after making an exit hole in my window glass. (Guards have been removed for the purposes of illustration. Never operate a table saw without guards.)

the delivery of the finished piece. And, at every stage in the furniture making process — rough-cutting to length, ripping out, bandsawing, turning, sanding, finishing, etc. — the craftsman is making important decisions about how that material will be presented.

When you're selecting material in a lumber yard, you have to keep the ultimate application of that material in mind. Except for seat rungs and the bottoms of chair arms, every aspect of every part in a post-and-rung chair is visible. This means that a length of material that is cosmetically good on one side but not on the other simply won't do for most chairmaking applications, despite the fact that the same material might be perfectly acceptable for use as a tabletop, a use that permits the cosmetic defect to be placed on the bottom side. Most chair material must be cosmetically good through and through.

Even more important, because a chair must support not only its own weight but also the shifting weight of a human body, chair parts need to be fabricated from material with no structural defects. This means that a length of material having grain runout on one end is not appropriate for ripping into chair rung blanks, even though the material might have extraordinary color and figure.

After being ripped from a wider board, turning blanks will often exhibit a little bow. This stock needs to be straightened before it can be turned.

I straighten it on my jointer, aligning it so the side of the blank on which the two ends are "high" is flat on the jointer table. I then flatten the high ends as shown. Afterwards, in order to produce a square turning blank, I'll joint the adjacent face of the blank. If I don't do this, I end up with a blank that is a rectangle in cross section rather than a square.

This plank has been laid out so that it will yield rockers, slats, and arms. Since this particular plank is 1" thick, I know I can get two slat thicknesses and still have enough material to flatten and thickness the slat blanks.

While I reject a lot of material that might be good enough for casework, there is material that can be used for chair parts that could not be used for casework. For example, if I'm ripping up a length of maple into turning blanks and I see some checks on one end of a board that would prevent the material from being used as a table-top, I might be able to rip that piece into rung or post turning blanks by ripping between the checks.

Once you've assigned a piece of material to a particular use, for example, rockers, that doesn't signify the conclusion of the selection process. That process continues throughout the construction of a chair. Often, when I'm resawing stock for slats and rockers, the act of resawing will reveal a hidden defect, causing me to rethink what piece I will use where.

Several years ago, after quite a bit of head scratching, I figured out how to rip out all the parts for a Union Village rocker from a single, heavily-figured maple plank. (This chair appeared in my book *Authentic Shaker Furniture*.) All went well until I got to that part of the plank from

If I had a better band saw, I would resaw with a fence, but on my little machine, I get the best results resawing to a line.

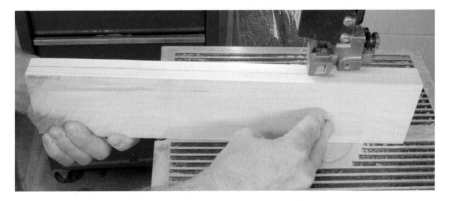

After straightening and flattening both sides of my slat blank, I can resaw the blank into two halves, each a bit more than $3/8$" thick — just enough to be dressed down to $1/4$", the thickness of the chair's slats.

Sometimes, no matter how careful I am at the planer, a board's finished surfaces reveal small areas of tear-out. These are best cleaned up with a card scraper as I'm doing here. I also use the scraper to remove planer snipe.

When the tear-out is too deep to remove by scraping, I'll try to layout the slat so that the torn-out area is either outside the slat shape or perhaps in the tenon section where it will mean nothing.

By carefully arranging my slat patterns, I'm able to avoid areas of tear-out or unsightly grain in my slat stock.

which I would resaw the two blanks for the rockers. When the two leaves fell apart on the table of my band saw, I was horrified to see a big tarry smear on either side of the cut. There was nothing on the outside of that board that hinted at the defect within. It was

simply there waiting to be revealed by my band saw. I was forced to use figured maple from another plank for those rockers.

Sometimes structural defects can be revealed when you open up a board. Recently, I've been plagued

with honeycombing (cavities in the wood caused by improper drying) in a load of 3"-thick walnut. Nothing on the outside of this material suggested the problems within, but once I started cutting the wood into turning blanks, the honeycombing was revealed.

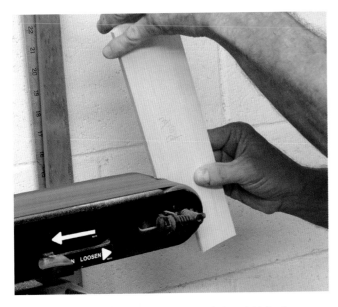

The open end on my stationary belt sander is just right for the cutouts on each end of the slats for the Union Village rocker.

I cut the rockers individually on my band saw.

I clamp the rockers together, fix them in a vise, and work the concave top edges of the rockers with a spokeshave.

I work the bottom edges of the rockers with a plane. These bottom edges don't have to be smooth to the touch since they will never be seen or touched, but they must have continuous curves without any flat spots that could interfere with smooth rocking.

The further you go in the chair-making process the further you refine the business of matching material to application. When you're looking at rung material, for example, it's important to remember that two of the chair's side rungs, one of the chair's front rungs and one of the chair's back rungs will be covered in seating material. This means that if you have some pieces without structural defects but with cosmetic defects, that material will make satisfactory seat rungs.

Sharpening Lathe Tools

Most of the chairs pictured in this book are primarily composed of lathe-turned parts. This means that some skill at the lathe is required. Fortunately, for those of us who are only average turners — a group that certainly includes me — it's possible to turn these parts without transcendent skill.

But, to perform on an *average* level, a craftsman must use tools exhibiting two characteristics: They must be sharp, and they must each have a single-ground bevel. Even if the cutting edge is sharp — if that sharpness was achieved by grinding a number of mini bevels — that tool will not perform as it should. So it's imperative that anyone who wishes to turn effectively pay close attention to the sharpening process.

Unlike plane irons, chisels and carving tools, many lathe tools can be taken directly from the grinder to the work. This is because the cutting edge of a lathe tool takes a tremendous battering at the lathe, and the ultra-sharp edges we apply to our

This is my wheel dresser in action, removing the top layer of abrasive along with the bits of heat-generating metal impacted in the layer.

This is the sharpening station in my shop. It is organized around two inexpensive dry grinders. Notice the after-market tool rest on the wheel on the extreme right. My wheel dresser sits to the left of the Black & Decker grinder. Diamond lapping plates and a Washita stone are positioned to the left of the dresser.

carving tools and plane irons would be quickly degraded in the production of turned work. This is a result of the fact that, in a single minute, the cutting edge on a lathe tool might remove 1,000" of shavings, whereas in a single minute, the cutting edge on a carving tool might remove only a couple inches of shavings. This is because the work in a lathe is spinning past the cutting edge of a tool at speeds of between several hundred to several thousand revolutions per minute.

The only exception to this straight-from-the-grinder rule in my shop is the skew. I'm constantly honing the tip, that part of the skew that sees the most action.

Sharpening Gear

One of the pleasures of teaching at a school like the Marc Adams School of Woodworking in Indianapolis is the opportunity it offers me to experiment with big-ticket power tools I will never own. It was here that I was first exposed to a Tormek grinder ($400 without lathe-tool accessories, which

This is my complete kit of turning tools, all with freshly ground bevels. At the bottom right is my favorite $1/2$" square skew that I bought at a garage sale. Next is a 1" skew, also a garage sale purchase, with a wider bevel than I typically grind. I've been experimenting with this bevel. Just above it is a new $3/4$" oval skew. The strange-looking creature above the oval skew is a Stanley chisel I reground for shaping rung tenons. (You'll see this tool in action later.) In the middle of the pack is another favorite, my 1" roughing gouge. Above that, a parting tool and $1/4$"- and $1/2$"-wide fingernail gouges.

In order to get tools that perform as they should, you need to know what they look like when they're properly sharp. This is my roughing gouge from above.

This is the bevel side of my roughing gouge. Notice that there is only one bevel. Many inexperienced turners work with tools having multiple bevels. This makes the use of the tools more difficult than it should be.

can add another $100 or so to the price tag) and a Oneway Wolverine jig. For readers who may be unfamiliar with the Wolverine, it's a jig designed to support long-handled lathe tools in a way that permits accurate bevel grinding on almost any grinder. It's moderately expensive ($80), but when used with even an inexpensive grinder, it makes it possible to get the kinds of bevels good lathe work requires.

However, while these sharpening aides are often clever and well made, it's important to remember that every gizmo designed to simplify the sharpening process provides its own complications. The Tormek is a wonderful tool, but you have to learn how to use it. The same can be said about the Wolverine or any other sharpening aide. Remember: Each one comes with an instruction book.

For that reason, I'm going to suggest that you consider my approach before you empty your wallet on an expensive sharpening system. My approach requires an expenditure of less than $150, a figure that includes the cost of two diamond lapping plates, a diamond slipstone, a good Washita stone, a two-wheeled grinder and a wheel dresser — sharpening essentials

that are not provided for in the quoted prices of a Tormek or a Wolverine.

(The equipment pictured on page 23 totals a bit more because I have a pair of two-wheeled grinders, but I could get by with just one.)

Grinders True and False
In the almost 40 years I've been building things from wood, and, in particular, the 20 years I've been writing about that process, I've encountered

more confusing and contradictory information about the business of sharpening tools than all other woodworking processes combined. Everybody agrees that you need sharp tools to do good work but there is almost no agreement about how best to attain those sharp tools and there is little agreement about what constitutes an appropriately sharp edge.

I think we need to begin by admitting that there's more than one way to skin this cat. A Tormek-based system will produce good results. A Wolverine-based system will produce good results. So will the one I'm about to propose, and so too will about a dozen other systems and approaches. It doesn't matter which route we choose, as long as we all arrive at the same destination — usable cutting edges at the ends of our tools.

If time were no object, we could do all of our cutting-edge shaping on stones, manually working our tools against various grits until we arrive at the proper shapes. But time is an object. No one wants to spend his or her entire weekend putting an edge on a turning skew. We want to arrive at that edge in a timely fashion

By keeping the gouge flat on my enlarged tool rest, you can see how the radius of the grinding wheel is being transferred to the bevel of my roughing gouge.

After I've feathered the edge of my roughing gouge down to nothing, I pull down the little burr on the inside of the gouge with my diamond slipstone. The burr will cut effectively until it falls away. The gouge then cuts with the sharp edge that remains behind.

so that we can spend our weekend using that skew to produce beautiful objects in wood. This means we need to enlist motorized assistance in the edge-forming process — namely — a grinding wheel.

Grinding wheels remove metal quickly, allowing us to reduce the amount of time required to shape the cutting edges of our tools. Unfortunately, the grinding process inevitably generates heat from the friction of one object — a grinding wheel — rubbing against another — the tool. Excessive heat degrades the metal in our tools, so, the first goal for anyone using a grinding wheel is reducing the heat the grinding process generates.

The advantage of a Tormek-type system is the presence of water. This allows us to keep our tools cool as we're creating the necessary cutting-edge shapes.

There are other ways to control the heat that builds up in cutting edges as we work them on a grinder. The most important of these is the frequent use of a wheel dresser.

When the surface of a wheel becomes clotted with the bits of metal it has ground from tools, it cuts less effectively, which means we must

hold a tool against it longer to create the desired edge, which means the process generates excessive friction heat. A wheel dresser solves that problem by grinding away the surface of the wheel, removing the bits of metal impacted in that surface, leaving behind a clean abrasive which will cut cleanly and quickly.

In his book *The Complete Guide to Sharpening*, Leonard Lee suggests that the wheels that come with inexpensive grinders are better suited for

use as paving stones than for grinding edges on woodworking tools. He suggests replacing those wheels with wheels designed for use on woodworking tools. He knows far more than I will ever know about grinding wheels, but my experience is that, although they may not be ideal, the wheels with which these grinders are equipped will work well if they are kept clean and used with common sense.

Grinder Common Sense

Effective work with a dry grinder requires two things: A light touch and constant movement. This is particularly true as we get closer to the finished shape, and the edge we're working gets thinner and thinner.

If you force a piece of tool steel against a wheel and hold it there, it certainly will heat up, and if we hold it there long enough, the heating will damage the metal in the cutting edge. It is possible, however, to be aggressive with an edge that is thick in cross section. For example, if you're shaping the edge of your skew and you've ground the cutting edge blunt to square it up, you can, at first, work those bevels aggressively. But, as you

Fingernail gouges require some extra effort to get them sharp without the multifaceted bevels you often see on the gouges of beginning turners. I begin with the gouge in this position, which allows me to construct a bevel on the left side of the gouge. The tool is flat on the rest even though it has been rotated slightly in the direction of its swing.

I keep the bevel of the fingernail gouge in contact with the wheel and swing the handle of the tool down as I slowly rotate the gouge so that when the handle reaches the bottom of its arc, the gouge is flat on its back on the tool rest.

I finish the stroke by swinging the handle of the gouge to the right while I rotate the gouge slightly in that same direction. You can see the single bevel on the cutting edge of the gouge.

approach the final thickness of your cutting edge, your touch must become lighter and you must keep the bevel moving across the face of the wheel so no individual section of the bevel is being pressed against the wheel continuously.

If you do this, you can easily dry-grind all of your turning tools without worrying too much about overheating them — with the exception of your roughing gouge.

The roughing gouge is the most important tool in your turning arsenal — at least it is in mine. I use it not only for roughing a square blank into a cylinder but also for much of my shaping. I use it to cut tapers on chair rungs and on the tops of front-post vases and on the bottoms of both front and back posts. (David Wright, a Windsor chairmaker, showed me a roughing gouge he had altered so that one side was a skew, giving him a tool of remarkable versatility.)

The roughing gouge can be fussy to grind. That's because the shape, a C in cross section, is difficult to manipulate on the grinder. This shape requires you to roll the gouge on your

grinding tool rest at the same time you're keeping it flat on the rest. I've addressed this problem by grinding the bevel in three sections. Each straight leg of the C is one section and the round between the legs is another. Handling the gouge in this fashion simplifies the tool's manipulation on my grinder's tool rest. But, even with this alteration of technique, the roughing gouge requires my fullest attention on the grinder in order to feather that bevel out to nothing without scorching the metal.

I should say something here about scorching the metal. As you practice grinding lathe tools, you might produce a smudge on your steel here and there as you approach the finished edges of your tools. If you do, don't panic. Simply lighten up your touch (and possibly dress your wheel). The metal in the smudged edge may be fractionally compromised, but it will cut just fine. In fact, I promise that you will not notice any decreased performance of that smudged edge as you work at the lathe. Please do not feel that you must grind the smudged metal away and re-form a bevel.

I have a can of water on the bench near my grinding wheel, but that water is not to save a scorched edge. Instead, I use the water to cool a part so I can handle it. If, for example, I'm grinding a bit of length from a bolt which I'm holding in a pair of pliers, I'll plop the bolt in the water so it will cool down enough to allow me to handle the bolt bare-handed.

I don't think it's possible to save the scorched edge of a tool when you're grinding a bevel. That's because it takes a couple of seconds for our brains to register the appearance of scorched metal, to send the message to our hands to move the part into the water and then to perform the movement. Unfortunately, it takes just milliseconds for heated metal to flicker through the color changes indicating excessive heating. By the time our brains have figured out what to do, the damage is already done. Sometimes I dip a part into the water prior to finish grinding because the water can buy me a couple of extra seconds on the wheel.

Grinding Wheel Tool Rest

In order to perform as it should, a lathe tool should have a single, hollow-ground bevel. The radius of that hollow grind is the radius of the wheel on which the bevel is ground. The photo at the bottom of page 24 shows how the positioning of the tool rest transfers the radius of the grinding wheel to the bevel of the tool being ground. In the case of a tool like a plane iron, you pass the tool back and forth across the tool rest while keeping the bevel in contact with the wheel. While the complicated shape of the cutting edges on turning tools requires a bit more planning, the fundamental concept is the same.

The problem with most dry grinders is that the factory tool rest is too small to allow you to keep the tool securely on the rest while passing it back and forth across the face of the wheel. To address this, I cut a couple rectangles of sheet steel and attached these rectangles to the factory tool rests with epoxy. (The photo at the top of page 23 shows an after-market rest on the left wheel of the GMC grinder.

These larger rests give you a secure bearing surface as you're grinding bevels. The wheel on the right side of the Black & Decker grinder has no rest because I use that wheel for miscellaneous free-hand grinding. The wheel on the other end of the Black & Decker has been replaced with a buffing wheel I charge with abrasives when I want an ultra-sharp cutting edge.

Lapping Plates

Forty years ago, when I first applied tools to wood, I sharpened those tools on a combination oilstone with a coarse grit on one side and a medium grit on the other. It worked reasonably well and produced usable edges on chisels and plane irons, as well as my pocket knife. But over time, the stone began to wear down in the middle, creating a hollow which rendered it all but unusable. This is a phenomenon you inevitably see in the collections of oilstones at antique malls or flea markets. The stones could be restored to usefulness by laboriously flattening the surfaces but those stones aren't worth the effort.

In the 1980s, when waterstones captured the imagination of the woodworking community, I tried a few, and, although they could be leveled easier than oilstones, I thought they were too soft to hold their shapes.

Then, in the 1990s, I discovered diamond abrasives. At first they were available only in small sizes. Several turners I know kept a couple of diamond paddles in their shirt pockets so they could quickly touch up an edge. The abrasives on these paddles were sharp and removed material quickly, but they were too small to do any real honing. What I wanted was the sharpness and durability of diamond abrasives but on a surface large enough to flatten the back of a tool.

Somebody must have been reading my mind because about five years ago, I saw diamond-impregnated steel lapping plates $2^1/2$" × $11^1/2$" in Woodcraft's catalog. These plates combined the two qualities I most wanted in my stones. The diamond abrasives cut quickly and remain sharp for years, and the steel plates to which they had been adhered could not be hollowed out by repeated honings. I immediately ordered the only grits they offered: 600 and 1200, as well as a diamond slipstone. I now use these plates for much of my back-flattening and honing work. If I'm honing a tool that requires a finer edge, I'll unpack my Arkansas stones, but I get very good performances from most tools that have been finish-honed by the 1200-grit diamond lapping plate.

The Stanley chisel I've reground for tenon forming is sharpened just like a plane iron. Here I'm flattening the back on a lapping plate.

Here I'm honing the edge of the chisel on the same lapping plate.

Turning Chair Parts

I t isn't necessary to be a great technician on the lathe in order to turn good chair parts in an efficient manner. I know because I do it every day.

Despite my 30 years of experience on the lathe, I'm only an average turner. Plus, because I'm left-handed and self-taught — even though I'm doing things the right way — my approach looks not quite like the approach of other experienced turners. I should probably also confess that I sand, a practice which is understandably disdained by some great

lathe technicians. I admire the transcendent skills of those technicians, but I have little interest in emulating their methods because my goal at the lathe isn't technical mastery; it's simply the production of good chair parts in an efficient manner. And fortunately, that's possible for someone like me with only average skills on the lathe.

This is an important point, particularly if you're new to the art of chairmaking, and you're intimidated by the prospect of mastering the lathe, a technically demanding tool. (I guess I should say "collection of tools"

because mastering the lathe means mastering the many tools associated with it. You can't, for example, master the lathe without also mastering the roughing gouge, the fingernail gouge, the skew and so on.)

If you want to learn classical lathe technique, there are lots of good books, videos and schools where you can work with instructors who have devoted their lives to achieving technical mastery. But if you want to learn to produce good quality chair parts in a minimum of time, you might want to look at the next few pages. But be warned — in addition to lathe technique, I'm going to give you the phone number of a company that sells rolls of abrasives which are perfect for lathe sanding.

As you read through this chapter, there are a couple of things I need to mention to make sure everything is clear to you. Because I work alone, it's difficult for me to get action shots that accurately demonstrate the concept I'm trying to explain. For that reason, most of the lathe technique photos were taken with the lathe turned off in order to be sure I got the proper work/tool alignment.

Also, when you're looking at the turning demonstration photos, please remember that I'm left-handed. If you're right-handed, you will likely want mirror images of the hand and tool alignments you see.

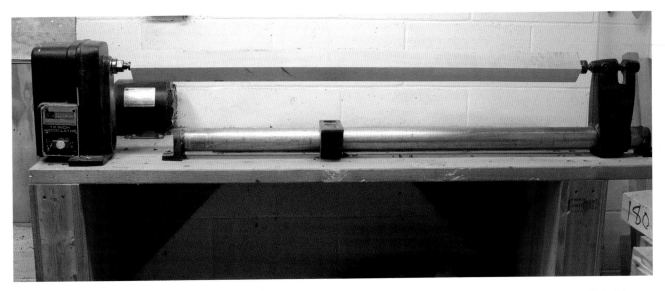

PHOTO 1 I customized this inexpensive Craftsman lathe to allow me to turn chair posts of more than 36" in length (a length standard for most consumer-grade lathes). The stand the lathe is mounted on is built around a pair of wood columns, each of which is filled with a couple of hundred pounds of gravel. This mass gives the lathe stability when turning a large part that may be slightly out of balance.

The Lathe

Consumer-grade lathes typically allow only 36" between centers. Unfortunately, that's not quite enough length for the back posts of most chairs. Most of the chairs in this book have back posts more than 40" in length and a couple are more than 44" long.

30 years ago, when I was first smitten with the desire to build chairs, I was astonished at the cost of lathes capable of taking more than 40" between centers. While I could buy a lathe at Sears for $220 that could be opened up to 36", the kind of lathes that could be opened an additional 10" were well over $1,000 at a time when $1,000 was quite a bit of money.

At that point in my life, my wife and I simply couldn't afford to spend $2000 on a tool that might never pay for itself, and for a while it looked as if my dream of making chairs was going to be pushed aside because we didn't have the money a good lathe required.

Finally, after several weeks of studying the problem, I had an idea. I would buy the inexpensive Sears lathe, order an extra mounting foot for the tubular steel bed, pull that bed out of its housing in the headstock, insert

the pulled end into the extra mounting foot, and, in that manner, create a lathe with a theoretically infinite distance between centers. Because the headstock and the tailstock were now essentially unconnected, I could turn anything I wanted as long as I built a bench long enough to accept the two ends of the lathe (see photo 1).

Because the mount for the Sears tool rest rode on the lathe's tubular lathe bed — which no longer ran beneath the full length of the parts I was turning — I also had to create a tool rest to cover the gap between the headstock and the beginning of the lathe bed. This got me thinking about

the whole idea of tool rests. Since I was going to have to build a tool rest to cover this short section of turned work, why not build length-of-part rests that would allow me to work along the entire length of the parts I was turning without moving the tool rest? This unexpected consequence of my lathe modifications turned out to be one of the most important elements of my approach to the turning of chair parts (see photo 2).

Safety

I don't spend a lot of time thinking about safety at the lathe. That's because in my 30 years of working

PHOTO 2 I've made a number of length-of-part tool rests that allow me to work along the entire length of a part without moving my tool rest.

29

with the tool I've established what I believe to be pretty good habits:

- I never turn on the lathe unless I'm wearing safety glasses.
- I never turn on the lathe if I'm wearing any loose clothing that might get hung up on the spinning part.
- I never turn on the lathe unless I've inspected the part for defects.
- I never turn on the lathe unless I've double-checked to see that the part is securely snugged up between centers and that the part will clear the tool rest through a 360° rotation. Then, when I'm actually turning, I'm protected by other similarly good habits:
- I never engage my tool with the work unless that tool is securely situated on my rest.
- I never use any part of my cutting edge that is not supported by the rest. (For example, I won't allow the heel of my skew to engage the work if that heel is sitting 1/2" above the rest. If I do, the heel of the skew will be slammed down onto the rest with enough force to startle me and perhaps set in motion a dangerous chain of events.)
- Even though I often use the palm of my off hand as a steady rest, I never wrap my fingers around the part, a grip which could cause my fingers to be drawn up into the gap between the spinning part and the tool rest.
- Most important, I never begin a turning sequence unless I've first reviewed it in my mind so that I can work out any problems before I start to work on the actual part.

I've never been hurt on the lathe, but I have had a couple of near misses. One incident occurred maybe 40 years ago when I was turning a fat candlestand on my dad's lathe. It wasn't my very first time on the tool, but it was one of my first times. Nevertheless, I thought I knew what I was doing. I'd reviewed, but not read, the tool's instruction book, and I considered myself to be pretty handy in the shop.

I mounted the 6" × 6" × 24" laminated walnut turning blank. I tightened up the tailstock and gave the part a jiggle to check that it was securely mounted.

Then I turned on the lathe.

I don't know exactly what happened in the next two seconds because it happened too fast for my brain to make a record, but I could reconstruct the events by examining the damage.

I had forgotten to turn the part all the way around to see that all four of its corners cleared the tool rest. One did not, which broke in half the cast-iron tool rest and tore the turning blank from its position between centers, sending it skittering across the lathe and onto the floor, somehow missing my body, despite the fact that I was foolishly standing there next to the machine as if I'd taped a "Hit Me" sign to my shirt.

On another day, maybe 15 years later, I was turning a back post for a chair when the tailstock broke loose from the lathe bed, the 45" turning blank broke free and cart-wheeled across my shop. I wasn't hurt, but once again, events unfolded too quickly for me to take useful defensive

action. It was only good luck that kept that part from rearranging my teeth.

Speed is the lesson in both stories. When something goes wrong at the lathe, it goes wrong in a hurry, much too fast for the useful intervention of human reflexes. There's no time to consider how to best defend yourself and there's no time for evasive action. That's why it's imperative that you plan safety into your turning regimen and that you mentally rehearse tricky sequences in advance, eliminating any steps that seem risky.

Turning Stock

All turning stock should be as free from defects as possible because every knot, every check, every bit of boggy wood has within it the potential for disaster when it's spinning at 1350 rpm in your lathe.

Knots can catch a tool, ripping out a chunk of wood, and if you encounter a knot at a moment when your attention is wandering, the encounter can wrest your tool from your hands.

Checks are particularly dangerous because they can come apart without warning. This has happened to me several times when the checks were very faint and my inspection

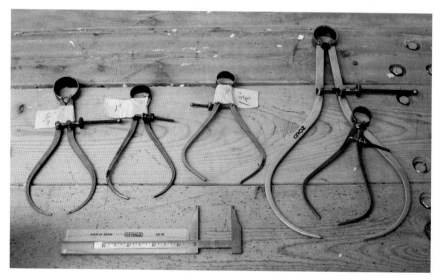

PHOTO 3 In order to make quick determinations of part diameters while a part is being turned, I have a couple dozen adjustable calipers, each of which is set to one of the diameters with which I most commonly work. The Stanley caliper at the bottom allows me to measure other diameters.

insufficient, but, fortunately, nothing scary happened. Sections of the parts simply fell away, but the potential for disaster was present.

The term *boggy* wood refers to anything that's not sound because of water damage or insect infestation. I avoid such material because I never know how it's going to behave in the lathe. But, I should also mention that several years ago, for *Woodwork* magazine, I profiled a turner named Mark Burhans, who works almost exclusively with spalted wood, and Mark said he had never had problems with material coming apart in the lathe.

You should also be aware of grain runout when you're selecting material for chair parts. The strongest parts are those in which the grain runs continuously from end to end. And, when you plan to bend a part, for instance, a chair's back post, it's essential to pick material without grain runout.

Turning Preparation

In addition to the edge tools I discussed in the previous chapter, I keep a number of measuring tools with me at the lathe. Most are unmarked adjustable calipers (see photo 3).

I have about 20 sets of these calipers, each one adjusted to register one of the diameters with which I commonly work. For example, nearly all the rung tenons on my chairs have a diameter of $5/8$", so one set of calipers is set to register that diameter. Another is set to $1^3/8$", the most common diameter for the posts of New Lebanon chairs. Another is set to $15/16$", the maximum diameter of a New Lebanon rung — at least the way I make that rung. These calipers are set to register a certain amount of resistance when they are placed over a spinning part, an amount of resistance I have trained myself to recall.

If the $5/8$" calipers won't go over a spinning rung tenon, I know it's grossly oversized. If it fits over a spin-

ning rung tenon in a sloppy manner, I know the tenon is undersized and the part must be scrapped. But if it passes over the spinning tenon firmly with moderate resistance, I know the tenon is good.

While you may at first want to stop the lathe every time you check a diameter, using perhaps a set of calipers on which measurements are marked on a scale, eventually you will realize that you can't get anything done if you are continually shutting off the lathe to make these checks. Typically, I'll make a dozen diameter checks during the turning of a single rung, mostly on the tenons. In fact, I probably spend more clock time checking diameters than I do turning those diameters.

I do, however, have one set of calipers — the Stanley calipers at the bottom of photo 3 — with which I can measure a diameter if I'm dealing with a non-standard part.

For years, I made square turning blanks into octagons before mounting them in the lathe, thinking that this made the turning process a little less stressful. The idea wasn't mine. I stole it from another chairmaker I very much respect, but the process required the use of a couple of bandsaw jigs and a great deal of time, in addition to some wear and tear on my band saw. However, a friend who visited my shop on a day when I was making octagons scoffed at the process which he characterized as unnecessary. I thought about his judgment after he left and decided he was right. What a waste of time. I can turn that square post blank into a cylinder in just a few seconds on the lathe, while it may take me five minutes to band saw a square post blank into an octagon, to say nothing of the set-up time the fussy octagon-making jig requires.

Before you can mount a turning blank on your lathe, you must locate

the end-grain centers of that blank, and, if you're using a spur center on the headstock end of your lathe, as I do, you must also incise an X in the end grain to give the spur center something to grip. I do these things simultaneously on my band saw.

My band saw table has a notch extending from the front of the blade to the front edge of the table. This notch allows me to install new blades on my band saw. It can also be used to locate the bottom corner of a turning blank when I'm marking centers. I simply align one corner of the blank in the notch, hold the blank so that the blade meets the opposite corner and press the blank into the running band saw blade to cut an incised diagonal. I repeat the process to create the second diagonal, and the end-grain center of the blank is the place where these two bandsawn incisions intersect (see photo 4).

Once the blank is centered, I start a hole for each lathe center, tapping the point of an awl into the center of each end of the blank which I then mount in the lathe, snugging up the tailstock so there is enough pressure on the blank to cause the spurs in my drive center to engage with the end grain. I then rotate the blank by hand

PHOTO 4 I locate centers of turning stock by incising diagonals on the ends of the stock using my bandsaw..

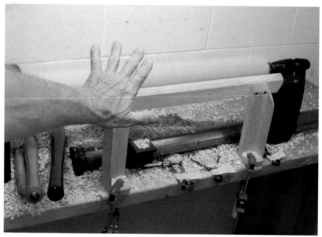

PHOTO 5 The corners of a turning blank should clear the rest by at least $^1/_8$". Be sure to rotate the blank a full 360° before turning on your lathe.

PHOTO 6 When I turn on the lathe with a freshly mounted blank, I stand back and hold my hand in front of my face to protect myself against the unlikely event of a blank coming apart.

(see photo 5) to ensure that the blank won't strike the rest when the lathe is turned on.

The rest should clear the blank by at least $^1/_8$".

I do nearly all of my spindle turning at 1350 rpm. I suspect that's faster than many lathe instructors would recommend, but I've been turning chair parts for many years at that speed and I'm quite comfortable with it. I also believe that the tendency of long thin spindles to whip in the lathe (more later) is reduced at a relatively high speed.

When the part is securely installed between centers — after I've checked to see that the part clears the rest — I turn on the lathe, holding one hand as shown (see photo 6). I don't always perform this little act of workshop safety, but I do whenever I have a spindle that I suspect might be a bit unbalanced. I put out my hand because I would rather a careening part strike my hand than my head.

The Roughing Gouge Dance

I have experimented with walking along the length of the back posts I'm turning with my roughing gouge in my hands, sliding it along the tool rest while it's engaged with the work, but

the walking process jars my arms and hands out of alignment, which compromises the work. As a result, I've resigned myself to turning each back post in two, 20"- 24" sections, the maximum distance I can comfortably manage without moving my feet.

It's important that the hand/tool alignment remain constant as you work your way along a turned part. If

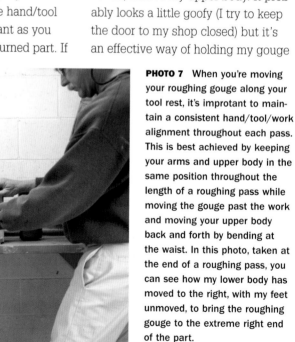

you start moving your arms to slide the tool toward you and to push it from you, you'll lose the alignment of the bevel, cutting edge and part that is necessary for working at the lathe.

So instead of moving my arms and hands, I move my upper body. It probably looks a little goofy (I try to keep the door to my shop closed) but it's an effective way of holding my gouge

PHOTO 7 When you're moving your roughing gouge along your tool rest, it's important to maintain a consistent hand/tool/work alignment throughout each pass. This is best achieved by keeping your arms and upper body in the same position throughout the length of a roughing pass while moving the gouge past the work and moving your upper body back and forth by bending at the waist. In this photo, taken at the end of a roughing pass, you can see how my lower body has moved to the right, with my feet unmoved, to bring the roughing gouge to the extreme right end of the part.

PHOTO 8 In this photo, I'm at the other end of a pass.

so I can quickly cylinderize a square turning blank.

Because I'm left-handed, I begin my roughing work by positioning my feet at the right end of the part I'm turning. In fact, an imaginary line extended from the right-hand end of the part I'm turning to the floor would fall about midway between my feet (see photo 7). I then tilt my upper body forward, bending at the waist, as I scoot the roughing gouge along the tool rest ahead of me, taking care to keep my upper body in a consistent alignment. My feet don't move, and neither does my upper body. I then roll the gouge over and lean back, pulling the gouge along with me, keeping my upper body in exactly the same position (see photo 8).

When I'm doing my roughing-gouge dance, the only part of my body that moves is my waist.

Riding the Bevel

There are two basic approaches to lathe work: cutting and scraping. I

know next to nothing about scraping because it doesn't appear to have much use in the turning of the kinds of parts my chairs require (although I should confess that in the past I have used my cutting tools to scrape out shapes I didn't know how to produce using a cutting action). Scraping tools — at least as I understand them — are used with their backs flat on the rest, which at first glance makes scraping seem so much simpler than cutting. After all, if you're scraping out a cove, all you need to do is push a gouge of the correct shape into the spindle you're working. The problem with scraped shapes is that they take more time to form and they leave surfaces requiring lots of sanding. Cut shapes, on the other hand, require much less time and sanding. In the hands of great lathe technicians, cut shapes may require no sanding at all.

In Chapter 3, I stressed the importance of grinding the bevels of turning tools with a single bevel. (Obviously, skews and parting tools will have single bevels on both sides of their cutting edges.) I said this not because a single bevel produces a sharper edge than several mini-bevels can produce, because it's possible to produce a sharp cutting edge with mini-bevels. The reason for working with a single bevel is this: A single bevel can ride securely on the spinning work, a configuration of tool and work, which gives you maximum control of the tool when it's used with a cutting rather than a scraping action.

Novices often push their lathe tools into the work in order to get the tools to cut, and the tools will cut if used in this manner, but pushing causes problems,

not the least of which is chatter, which can result from the stressed spindle bouncing against the tool's cutting edge. You can avoid this problem from the moment you first present your roughing gouge to the work if you keep in mind the idea of resting the tool's bevel on the cylinder. This is, perhaps oddly, true even before there is an actual cylinder on which that bevel can ride.

To bring the bevel of your roughing gouge to rest on the as-yet-not-formed cylinder, simply lay the heel of the bevel on the spinning work (it will bounce a little on the square corners of your turning blank) and gently pull the tool toward you as you simultaneously raise the tool's handle. The cutting edge barely engages the work and sends a jet of chips into the air.

This tool/work engagement should be done gently. There's no reason to push the tool into the work in an effort to make it cut. You control the cutting action by raising and lowering the handle a little. When you raise it up, the cutting edge engages the work and creates chips. When you lower the handle, the cutting edge disengages, and the flow of chips stops. At no point in this process should there be any forward thrust of the tool into the work.

Before you go any further with your first roughing session, with the lathe on, practice raising and lowering the gouge to start and stop the flow of chips.

Once you've developed a feel for this aspect of roughing gouge use, it's time to consider your grip on the tool.

Most instructors suggest that you cradle the roughing gouge in your hand from underneath. Because I'm self taught, I use a different grip (see photo 9), with my left hand laid gently over the gouge to hold the alignment.

With this alignment, I'm using the sway of my upper body to push the gouge forward in the direction of

PHOTO 9 To keep my fingers clear of my tool rest supports, I frequently use this grip on my roughing gouge. I establish the correct cutting edge/work interface by first resting the heel of my gouge on the spinning work. Then I draw the tool back toward me as I simultaneously raise the handle until a stream of chips begin to flow from the cutting edge. There is no forward thrust of my gouge into the work.

the headstock. When I reach the end of the stroke, I'll roll the gouge back toward my body about 90° and use the sway of my upper body to pull the gouge toward the tailstock end of the lathe. In both directions, the gouge is lifting chips from the turning with the flat, bottom section of the cutting edge immediately beside the curve of the gouge's cutting edge. (I don't think I've ever used the curved section of the gouge's cutting edge.)

I also use the forward sway of my upper body to push the gouge toward the lathe's headstock, but sometimes I use an alternative grip on the tool (see photo 10), one that allows me to support the back side of a thin spindle with the palm of my hand.

I once again use the sway of my upper body to draw the gouge toward the tailstock, but in this case (see photo 11), I'm also using the palm of my hand to support the thin spindle.

PHOTO 10 This is an alternate grip I use when I want to support the back side of a thin spindle with the palm of my hand.

How Sharp is That Gouge?

When you're learning to turn, it's hard to make a useful determination of sharpness simply by rubbing your thumb across the cutting edge. Because these edges are intended for the battering they will receive on the lathe, they aren't going to possess the dangerous sharpness of a smoothing plane iron or a carving gouge. Turning tools need only to be sharp enough to lift chips from lathe-turned work, so the only useful test of a turning tool's sharpness is the way it cuts the stock mounted in your lathe, and one of the easiest ways to test a tool's cutting action is to examine the shavings the tool produces.

The first shavings your gouge removes from a square turning blank will be small. Once the blank has been cylinderized and you have the roughing gouge's bevel riding securely on the turning (see photo 12), the gouge should be producing long, looping noodles of shavings. At that point, if you're still getting chips and sawdust, something is wrong with either your presentation of the cutting edge to the work or the sharpness of that cutting edge.

Take a look at the shavings in photo 13. If your shavings don't look like that, it's time to troubleshoot.

First, review the way you're presenting the tool to the work. Make sure you're achieving a cutting action by placing the heel of the bevel on the spinning work and then raising the gouge's handle in order to engage the cutting edge. Make sure that you're not pushing the tool into the work.

If you determine that your technique is solid, the cutting edge is the likely culprit, so you need to make another trip to the grinder. Please don't get frustrated because, if you're a novice turner, you will almost certainly need to take a few trips back and forth from the lathe to the grinder before you get a cutting edge that performs the way it should. Even when you're taking light passes, you should be cutting noodles, not dust.

A Vocabulary of Shapes

In order to decide how you're going to create the shapes a particular turning requires, first, mentally break down those shapes into their basic elements. Different turners use different vocabularies to denote their lists of basic shapes. My list is as follows: end-grain parings, tapers, flats, beads and coves.

Every turning I've ever created was made up of some combination of these elements. The vase under the arm of a New Lebanon chair, for example, consists of a half bead at the base with a taper above the vase's swelling and a square shoulder at the base of the tenon on the top of the vase. So, when I'm turning this vase, I don't think vase and then tenon. I think half-bead, swelling, taper, end-grain paring and flat (for the tenon).

I reduce relatively complicated turnings to these basic elements. On the painted colonial desk (see photo 15), you'll see a number of shapes on each leg. Starting at the bottom of the leg's foot, I translated those shapes

PHOTO 11 In the previous photo I showed the grip I use when to support the back of a thin spindle when the gouge is being pushed toward the head stock. In this photo, I'm demonstrating the grip I use when I'm supporting the back of a thin spindle as I'm drawing the gouge toward me and the tailstock.

PHOTO 12 This is another grip I use when drawing the gouge toward the tailstock. You can see how the bevel rides on the turning.

35

into the following list: taper, end-grain paring, bead, end-grain paring, cove, end-grain paring, full bead and half bead which widens into the leg's bottom-most square section. This provided me with a plan of attack for producing those shapes. It told me how I would hold my tools and how I would manipulate them at each stop along the creation of the leg's foot.

1. End-grain Paring

I use this simple shape element at some point on most of my turned parts. For example, I use it to clean up the tiny shoulders adjacent to the tenons on my New Lebanon reproductions. This technique is not only used for cuts that are perfectly perpendicular to the part's axis of rotation. It can also be used to create crowned shapes, like the top of a side chair's front post.

Before you make this cut at the top of a post, you must clear out space on the turned part for your skew to perform its work. I do this by working my roughing gouge on the waste side as close to the intended position of the cut as possible. I then switch to my $1/2$" skew and make a number of rough paring cuts on both sides of the final cut, the waste side as well as the post side. (The waste side cuts are needed only to create space for the skew to operate on the good side.)

The end-grain paring cut requires a narrow skew with a fairly steep grind on either side. I've experimented with wider skews having the long, shallow angles on their bevels many craftsmen prefer, but those skews have a tendency to run down the turning damaging or destroying the part by incising a deep spiraling cut. Unfortunately, there is no way to stop your skew once it starts to go since the whole run takes place in a fraction of a second. By the time your brain alerts you to the problem, the skew has completed its run.

PHOTO 13   Probably the best way for a novice turner to assess his or her technique at the lathe and the grinder is by examining the shavings. Once a blank has been rendered round, the shavings should be long, looping noodles of wood. If they're sawdust at that point, something needs to be changed. Either the technique should be adjusted or, more probably, the tool should be sharpened.

PHOTO 14   Even light passes taken from thin spindles should result in long shavings like these seen here.

It is possible for a properly ground $1/2$" skew to run down your part when you're using it to pare end grain if you're not careful about how you engage the work with the skew's cutting edge. This particular cut must be made with only the very tip of the skew, and it must be made with the skew tilted slightly away from the end-grain form you're paring. If any part of the skew's cutting edge, other than the tip, engages that end-grain surface, the skew will catch and dig up your work and startle you as well.

That's why I would recommend practicing this cut on a scrap turning (this suggestion applies to all the other cuts I'm going to discuss) before you attempt it on an actual chair part.

This technique is important because it leaves smooth end-grain surfaces requiring no sanding — surfaces you can't achieve with any scraping method I've ever tried. To achieve the very best end-grain surfaces, you should rough in the shape with several relatively heavy passes, then finish up with one or two light passes with your skew.

2. Tapers

The frequent use of tapers is one of the hallmarks of turned Shaker parts. Rungs often taper from a thick middle to small shoulders adjacent to the tenons on both ends of the rung. The bottoms of both front and back posts taper along their bottom-most sections, and back posts typically taper upward from just above the seat rung to the finial at the top of the post.

Fortunately, tapers are the easiest elements in my vocabulary to create. I form them with my roughing gouge by taking more and heavier passes from those sections of a part that will end up with the smallest diameter. For example, if I'm cutting the tapers on a rung, I start by forming the tenon on either end. I then take multiple passes with my roughing gouge from the direction of the rung's center to the shoulder adjacent to the tenon. The first pass on one end might begin at the middle of the rung's length. The next might begin an inch from that middle closer to the tenon. The third might begin three inches from the middle. Also, on each pass, I'll raise the gouge's handle a bit as I near the tenon, which causes the gouge to take an increasingly thick shaving.

Once I've roughed in both tapers, I step back, checking to see if they're balanced and correct any imbalances.

PHOTO 15 Every turning I do is broken up into a series of very simple shapes. This is true even when the turnings are as complex as the legs on this desk.

PHOTO 16 It's possible to make clean end-grain cuts when you use the very tip of a skew.

3. Flats

Sometimes a turning will include a narrow flat between a couple of other turned elements. Flats of this type are best executed with a parting tool, as I'm demonstrating in photo 17. Start the cut by resting your parting tool on its edge on the tool rest with the heel of its bevel riding on the work. Then gradually draw the tool toward you while simultaneously raising the handle of the parting tool until it begins to take a shaving. The parting tool will quickly burrow into the turning, leaving behind a narrow flat. You can create wider flats by making repeated cuts with your parting tool.

In the practice of post-and-rung chairmaking, the most important flats are the sides of the round rung tenons that will be fit into round mortises when the chair is assembled. While these tenons can be formed with repeated passes of a parting tool as described above, I've developed a better method using the odd-shaped butt chisel appearing in Photo 20.

I demonstrate this method every year in the chairmaking classes I teach at the Marc Adams School, and while most of my students adopt my method, some experiment with alternatives, including repeated passes with a parting tool, which, although slow, is effective.

Others bring the tenons to the approximate diameter with a roughing gouge and then finish the sizing using a skew chisel with a planing action. Herb Pfundt, who was volunteering that summer to work with me as an assistant instructor, once brought in a set of rounders. These are English tools designed for the specific purpose of fashioning round tenons, and while I enjoyed seeing the rounders doing their work, using them to create the many tenons a chair requires seemed to me to be an unnecessary complication. It's so much simpler to create the tenons on the lathe at the same time

PHOTO 17 A parting tool can be used to create a narrow flat between two other elements.

you're creating the other elements of the rungs.

My method begins with the conversion of a rung blank to a cylinder with a roughing gouge. Then, I mark off the shoulders for the rung's two tenons using my skew standing on edge upside down to incise fairly deep marks in the rough cylinder as shown in photo 18.

Next, using my $1/2$" fingernail gouge, I hollow out the center of the portion that will be the tenon, using my eye to tell me when the smallest

diameter of the hollow is approximately $5/8$". (See photo 19.)

With the lathe still on, I check that diameter with my preset $5/8$" caliper. If the caliper passes over the hollow with the proper feel, I begin to create the actual tenon with a Stanley butt chisel I have ground for that particular purpose.

There's little risk of turning a tenon undersize with this process. If the thinnest section of the hollow is a bit less than $5/8$", I simply bring the rest of the tenon to $5/8$", leaving

PHOTO 18 Since it is the joint formed by the union of round tenon and round mortise that provides the chair with its strength, one of the most important aspects of turning post-and-rung chair parts is the turning of the rung tenons. I begin a tenon by marking the shoulder with a skew standing on edge as shown here.

PHOTO 19 With a fingernail gouge, I hollow out the tenon until it looks right. I then check the diameter with a set of calipers preset to $5/8$".

PHOTO 20 When the least diameter of the hollow is $5/8$", I use a wide butt chisel bevel-side down to establish the entire length of the tenon.

a narrow band that is less than $5/8$", which causes no problems at assembly whatsoever.

For several years I formed those tenons with a non-customized butt chisel, but the bevels on each side of the chisel sometimes caused the chisel to tip in use. So, I finally ground away the beveled areas on each side of the chisel, leaving me with a 1"-wide central section without any bevels to cause tipping.

To finish a tenon with this tool, I lay the chisel bevel-side down on my tool rest, with the heel of the bevel resting on the tenon. I then raise the handle of the chisel while simultaneously drawing the chisel slightly toward me. This engages the chisel's cutting edge with the tenon section I have just hollowed out. If the chisel is sharp enough, it produces a clean straight-sided tenon. (See photo 20.)

Using my $1/2$" skew, I cut a slight taper on the end of the tenon to allow it to slip more easily into its mortise at assembly. (See photo 21.) I then make an end-grain paring cut on the tenon's shoulder to clean up any loose fibers.

4. Beads

I use my $1/2$" skew to create beads and half beads as shown in photos

PHOTO 21 I finish up the tenon by cutting a slight bevel on the end to make it easier for the tenon to slide into its mortise without getting stuck. (Later, after the rest of the rung is turned, I'll clean up the shoulder with an end-grain paring cut.)

PHOTO 22 I randomly established some lines on this test spindle to mark locations and limits for a pair of half beads and a cove.

22-25. For the purpose of this bead-and-cove demonstration, I started by randomly placing a few lines on a roughed-in cylinder to mark the intersection of a pair of half beads, as well as the limits of a cove. (See photo 22.)

I begin the pair of half beads by using my skew, on edge and upside down, to incise a deep cut in the roughed in cylinder as shown as shown in photo 23. This cut marks the point where this pair of half beads

PHOTO 23 I begin a half bead by incising a line with a skew stood on edge.

PHOTO 24 With the skew laid nearly flat on the rest, I start a cut about ¼" from the incised line and then roll the tip of the skew into the incision.

comes together. I begin to make a number of rolling end-grain paring cuts, using only the very tip of my skew (this is essentially the same technique I demonstrated in my end-grain paring section). The first cut starts less than ¼" from the incised line, with the skew tilted away from the line and the flat of the skew almost parallel with the surface of the turning. I engage the tip of the skew and keep it engaged so it pushes ahead a little roll of shaving. I roll the skew toward the incised line so the skew is standing on its edge in the position it was in when it incised the initial line. (See photo 24.) I finish the half bead by making several of these passes, each time pushing ahead a little roll of shaving. (See photo 25.)

The specific contour of the bead is determined by the manner in which the skew is manipulated. It's possible to create a bead that is relatively flat on top with a sharp curve descending toward the incised cut. It's also possible to create a bead more rounded on top with relatively flat curves descending toward the incised cut.

If you want a full bead, you simply cut a mirror-image half bead at an appropriate distance from the one you just finished.

Novice turners sometimes scrape out a shape like this (I know I did) because they find the cutting process intimidating. However, the sanding necessary to clean up the tearout caused by scraping can change the shape of the bead. Cut beads require little work with abrasives. I lightly sand to create the smoothly flowing lines I want my beads to have. A great

PHOTO 25 After making several passes, each one progressively farther from the incised line, I have a finished half bead. The size and depth of the bead can be increased by making more rolling passes with my skew, and a whole bead can be fashioned by creating a mirror-image second half-bead an appropriate distance from the first.

PHOTO 26 I start a cove by standing my fingernail gouge on its side with the flute facing the cove I'm going to cut.

PHOTO 27 Next, I roll the gouge into the cove with an action that is a little like scooping, taking pains to keep the gouge's bevel tight against the work.

turning technician, however, can create those lines using only his skew.

5. Coves

I begin the creation of a cove by standing a fingernail gouge on its edge, with the flute of the gouge facing the cove I'm about to cut (see photo 26). I then press the tip of the gouge into the work and immediately roll the bottom of the gouge into the cove with a motion that is a little like scooping. If I keep the bevel pressed against the work, the gouge cuts, rather than scrapes, leaving behind a clean surface that requires little sanding. (See photo 27.)

A word of warning. This cut should be practiced on scrap before you attempt it on a part you hope to use. If you're hesitant and uncertain as you roll your gouge into the work, the gouge will skitter away from the cove along the turning, defiling the spindle. (I'm not suggesting that the gouge can read your mind and punish your lack of confidence, but there is something in the physics of this cut that rewards authority and punishes hesitation. Also, when the gouge takes off, it's always in the direction of the gouge's bevel.)

To create a cove, you should work from both sides toward the middle, widening and deepening the cove a bit at a time.

The reward for mastering this technique is a clean, almost-ready-for-finish surface. The finished cove (see photo 28) has no tearout, even in an irascible species like curly maple. (The finished half beads on the left, cut using my $1/2$" skew, are also clean.)

6. Finials

Finials require special attention because they typically occur at the

PHOTO 28 As you can see, little sanding is required to finish either the cove or the two half beads.

ends of long spindles, which have a tendency to whip in the lathe. This can cause a slender part to come apart with disastrous results.

When I'm turning a back post with a finial having elements slender enough to be fragile, I have a sequence I've developed for producing that back post that presents little risk of the finial breaking. First, I turn the part unshaped, leaving the finial oversized. In the case of the acorn finial (see photo 29), I leave the cove beneath the acorn with a diameter of about $3/4$" and the waste attached to the top of the acorn turned to about the same diameter. I sand the rest of the part and mark it while it's still in the lathe.

When everything else is done, I turn my attention to the finial. I reduce the diameter of the cove below the acorn to its final thickness, then pare off more thickness in the waste at the top of the acorn. I do this while using my off hand as a steady rest. Then I take the part from the lathe and saw off the waste.

Photo 30 shows the finials for the tape-back No.5 that appears in this book. The top finial is fresh from the saw that removed the waste. The bottom finial has been handworked with a paring chisel, rasp and sandpaper to clean it up.

It takes some thinking to figure out how you're going to render the details of a finial. The button finial (see photo 31) is found on the top of the back post on the splint-back stool. The button required a $1/4$" fingernail gouge to cut the partial cove at the base of the nipple, while my $1/2$" skew was used to cut the bead-like form at the top of the nipple. The finial is nearly finished (see photo 31). All that remains is some clean-up with the $1/4$" gouge.

7. Sanding

As I said before, I sand at the lathe. I would prefer not to sand because the

PHOTO 29 I leave finial parts heavy until after I've sanded and marked the back post. Then I turn the finial parts down to their final diameters. I've reduced the cove below the acorn finial to its final size, and I've taken as much material as I can safely remove from the waste above the acorn.

PHOTO 30 The top finial is fresh from the saw that removed the waste tail. The bottom finial has been rasped and sanded to its final shape.

process throws dust into the air of my shop, but when I'm faced with a surface I can't finish any other way, I reach for the sandpaper. Nevertheless, I do everything I can to reduce the amount of time I spend sanding.

First, I use my skew and gouges to cut, rather than scrape, when I'm

producing coves and beads. But more important, I make use of a turner's best weapon in the war on sanding: I skew plane.

Most of the parts from which my chairs are assembled are simple. These shapes — primarily tapers — can be made with the roughing

The button finial at the top of the splint-back stool required some work with a $1/4$" fingernail gouge and my $1/2$" skew.

PHOTO 32 The top post in this photo is one of the back posts for the Union Village rocker in this book. The post mounted in the lathe is the partially turned second back post for that chair. As you can see, there is more than enough thickness in the finial section to yield the elements of the finial.

gouge, but even a careful use of a roughing gouge leaves behind minor surface irregularities. There are only two ways to clean up these irregularities: sanding and/or skew planing.

Skew planing is just what it sounds like. It's the practice of using a skew to smooth a turned part by the removal of cleansing shavings.

For many years, I've done my turning with only two skews, both of which are rectangular in cross section, but at the urging of friends, I recently added an oval skew to my tool kit for the specific purpose of planing and I like the way it performs.

I rest the skew on my tool rest with the bevel of the skew's cutting edge resting on the spinning work and the tool's long point at the top (see photo 36). The planing is done near the middle of the skew's cutting edge. To make the skew take a shaving, I do the same thing I do with a roughing gouge — I lift the tool's handle until the edge engages the work. You can see a shaving being lifted with my skew in the planing configuration (see photo 37). An alternative configuration (see photo 38) allows me to work in the opposite direction. This is necessary because planing — like all other lathe cutting actions — should always take place moving downhill.

Skew planing requires a light touch, constant attention to keep the shaving rising from the middle of the skew's cutting edge and good contact between the cutting edge's bevel and the spinning work. A brief lapse in concentration can cause the skew to dig in, taking more of a shaving than you intended.

I plane all my rungs, front posts and most other turned parts, but back

PHOTO 33 With a scored line, I marked the limit of the cove under the ball at the top of the finial. I also marked the limits of the ball and began to rough it into shape using the tip of my $1/2$" skew to pare across the end grain.

43

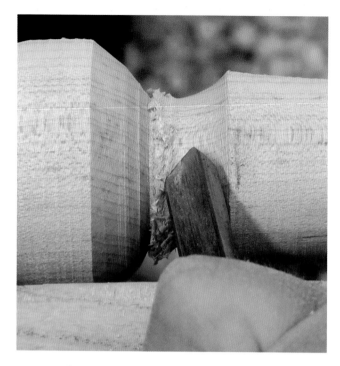

PHOTO 34   I remove waste from the cove, making sure that the bevel of my fingernail gouge remains snugged up to the work. This action produces a clean, end-grain cut.

PHOTO 35   Once the cove has been roughed in, I begin to refine the ball using the bead-forming technique.

posts, because they're so long and slender, tend to be whippy, which makes it harder to maintain the light touch skew planing requires. On good days, when my hands are feeling steady, I skew-plane my back posts as well, but on bad days, when it feels like I'm trying to control my tools with a pair of catcher's mitts, I sand my back posts.

I often find it necessary to sand other sections of my chair parts. For example, I'll sand where there's roughened grain between a section turned with a skew and a section turned with a gouge. Also, when forming a bead with my skew, I leave behind subtle planing marks that need to be removed by sanding.

The *Sanding Catalog*, (800-228-0000) offers high-quality rolls of sandpaper that are perfect for lathe sanding. I recommend the 2"-wide rolls as shown in photo 40. I often use 150- and 220-grits of paper. 100-grit paper is my backup paper for heavy sanding of chatter marks.

PHOTO 36   Skew planing removes most of the rough surface irregularities left by the roughing gouge. To engage the work, I lay the skew across the rest with the heel of the bevel on the work. I then draw the skew toward me while I'm simultaneously raising the handle of the skew until the cutting edge begins to take a shaving. I then push the skew forward along the spindle, taking care to keep the cutting edge engaged with the work.

8. Chatter

Chatter is what happens when a lathe tool bounces against the work, causing uneven and unsightly surfaces. Chatter marks appear as pockmarks, erratic widths in the track of a roughing gouge or as ridges that spiral, in an organized fashion, around a turned part. Spiraling can result from a long thin spindle being pushed out of line by aggressive turning, a breakdown at the end-grain centering for the tailstock or by a bit of hard or knotty wood.

Photo 42 shows the kind of chatter most commonly found in a post-and-rung chairmaking shop. These pockmarks are the result of a thin spindle being aggressively turned without the support of a steady rest. Notice the acceptable gouge marks on either end which gradually become pockmarks in the center where the spindle is most likely to flex away from the tool. Fortunately, most chatter episodes can be cured with a bit of lathe first aid.

Chatter Cure
The Steady Rest

My favorite steady rest is the one hanging from the end of my right arm, because it's so easy to install and to move to new positions. The disadvantage to using my off hand as a steady rest is the friction heating that occurs when the skin of my palm is rubbed by the spinning work. I used to manage this heating by wrapping the palm of my off hand with a few strands of masking tape, which works well as a heat sink, but it's inconvenient, so now I use my unprotected

PHOTO 37 When I'm planing thin spindles, I use this grip so I can support the back of the spindle with my hand.

PHOTO 38 This is the grip I use to support a thin spindle while drawing the skew toward me.

45

PHOTO 39 The skew produces a different kind of shaving than does a gouge.

PHOTO 40 Sometimes I need to sand a difficult section in order to get the surface I want. In such a situation, shop rolls like these from the *Sanding Catalog* are better than the best conventional paper.

hand, removing it for cool-downs when necessary.

If you choose this method, you must be careful about the gap between the tool rest and the work. If you wrap your fingers around the work, your fingers will be drawn up into that gap which can cause injury. It's best to make a conscious effort to dangle your fingers and touch the back of the work only with the palm of your hand.

If you use wraps of masking tape to protect your hand, be sure there are no loose strands that can catch on the spinning part. Remember: You can't move fast enough to hit the off-switch before the lathe can cause an injury.

Lighter Passes

This technique, when used in combination with a steady rest, can be effective with thin spindles.

Photo 43 shows the chattery spindle in photo 42 after using a steady rest and light passes. The result, as you can see, is a perfectly clean turning.

Hand Tool Work

Unchecked chatter gets worse. One chattery pass begets another, which begets another, each of which will likely be worse than the one that preceded it. If this syndrome goes on too long, you may not be able to rescue a chattery section using the two methods I described in the preceding text.

In such a case, you may want to work the area with hand tools to smooth out the surfaces enough to try a steady rest and/or a light pass. You can take a coarse rasp to a spinning part to subdue a difficult section, and then follow that up with a light pass with your lathe tool.

PHOTO 41 The deep gouge track in the center of this piece represents one kind of chatter, which is caused by the collision of the gouge's cutting edge with an ornery bit of grain.

PHOTO 42 The roughing gouge tracks on either end of this spindle are normal. However, the pockmarks in the center indicate that this spindle was turned too aggressively. The aggressive action of the roughing gouge deflected the spindle causing the cutting edge to vibrate against the work, which, in turn, caused the pocks.

PHOTO 43 The pockmarks in were eliminated by doing two things. First, I supported the back of the spindle with my off hand, and second, I took lighter passes with my roughing gouge.

Re-establish Tailstock Center

If the chattery part is rattling in the lathe, the chatter might be caused by a breakdown in the tailstock center. When a turning is under stress, particularly when you're knocking the corners off of a new part you just installed in your lathe, sometimes the point of the tailstock center will begin to enlarge the depression that the point has made in the part's end grain. If that has happened, no amount of rasp work or light passes or anything else will reduce the chatter until you've gotten the tailstock center re-established.

Making Arms

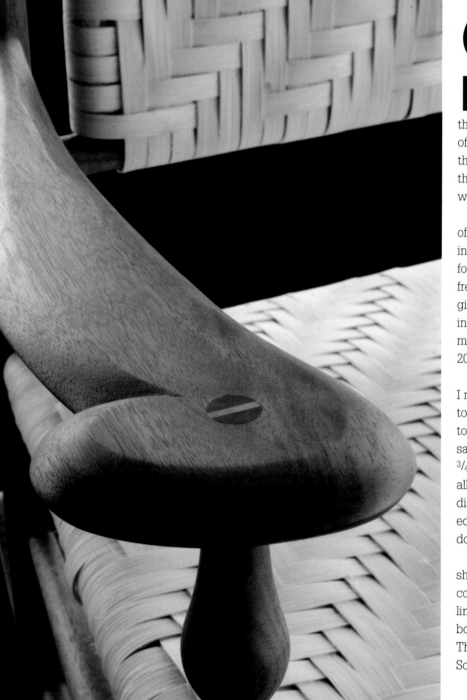

Some of the chairs I build are straight-forward reproductions of Shaker, Arts & Crafts and country originals. When I'm building these reproductions, I make the arms of these chairs exactly like those on the originals. Typically, this means that the arms will be simple cutouts with a gentle radius on the edges.

However, when I'm building chairs of my own design or when I'm building reproductions of historic originals for a customer who has given me the freedom to be a little expressive, I give the arms of the chairs I'm building some sculpture, using a hand-tool method I've developed over the last 20 years.

After I've bandsawn the arm blank, I mark it freehand on the top, the bottom and the edges. The line on the top should parallel the arm's bandsawn perimeter at a distance of about $3/4$". The line on the bottom also parallels the outside perimeter but at a distance of about $1/2$". The line on the edge is located about $3/5$ of the way down from the top surface of the arm.

Then, using a drawknife, a spokeshave, a rasp and carving tools, I connect the line on the top with the line on the edge and the line on the bottom with the line on the edge. The connecting surfaces form bevels. Sometimes, I cut these bevels with a

PHOTO 1 To define the top/bottom edge of the chair arm, you could fair the bandsawn edges before marking and make the line placement more precise by guiding the pencil with a try square or a jig, but I prefer to see this as a freehand process, one that requires me to be continually refining the perimeters of these bevels as I work them with shaving and carving tools.

PHOTO 2 The lines on the top surface of the arms are placed about $3/4$" from the bandsawn perimeter of the arm blank, while the line on the bottom will be placed about $1/2$" from that perimeter.

PHOTO 3 I use a pair of puppets that have been specially adapted for chair arms. On the inside of one puppet, I have a shallow $7/8$"-diameter mortise to receive the tenon on one end of the arm. (The tenon you use when you're pinning an arm blank between puppets should not be a tenon finished to $5/8$" in diameter. Instead, that tenon should be rough-shaped to about $3/4$". That's because the process of pinning the blank between puppets can deform the end of the tenon. You can cut away the deformed material when you're bringing that tenon to its final $5/8$" size.) On the inside of the opposite puppet, I've dished out a shallow area to receive the nose of the chair arm.

PHOTO 4 This photo shows the oversized tenon in the shallow mortise on the inside of one of the puppets. The starburst lines incised on the puppet's surface are the marks made by hundreds of drawknife strokes.

PHOTO 5 The nose of the arm from the Union Village rocker is fixed in the shallow depression on the inside of one of the puppets.

PHOTO 6 I'm using a drawknife to shape the arm for the Union Village rocker. The cut I'm making here is as close to the nose of the arm as I could get from this direction. To do further work on the opposite end of the arm, I need to move myself to the other end of the arm blank and work toward the other puppet.

slight crown. At other times, I make them relatively flat shapes.

Shaping a chair arm can be a challenge in itself. Part of the problem is gaining access to the parts of the arm you want to shape. It's almost impossible to work a part with a drawknife when that part is on a bench top or in a bench vise because there's no clearance for the handles of the drawknife. I've employed tools I call puppets, although I believe the English them poppets. (Copyeditor's note of interest: A poppet, in British usage, is a term of affection for a reliable person, based on the part of a boat used to pivot an oar.)

Puppets are blocks of wood mortised through to receive the 3/4" pipe of a pipe clamp. The pipe is fixed in a bench vise and a piece of work is pinned between the puppets using the pipe clamp head to provide tension. This raises the work above the bench top so there is room to operate

PHOTO 7 I'm using the drawknife to work a bevel on an arm from the walnut splint-back rocker. A finished arm sits on the bench.

PHOTO 8 While it's possible to use a drawknife to work across the end grain at the nose of the arm, it's easier to use a carving gouge at this location. Some of the gouge work is done with the blank between the puppets and the rest done when the arm is fixed on the bench top.

PHOTO 9 The shaping process progresses from the drawknife and the carving gouge, to the rasp and finishes up with sandpaper. These are the two rasps I use to refine the surfaces left by the drawknife and carving gouge. The brass-bristled brush allows me to clear impacted wood from the teeth of my rasp without dulling the teeth.

PHOTO 10 The drawknife and gouge leave behind relatively crude surfaces. The rasp is the first tool I use to refine those surfaces.

the handles of a drawknife without barking your knuckles.

Pinning a part between puppets isn't quite like fixing the part in a bench vise, and it takes some practice to learn how to work a part held in puppets. No matter how tight you draw up the pipe clamp head, a part can still be forced from its position between puppets if you apply enough lateral force. This means when you're pulling the knife toward you, you need to pull it in line with the pipe clamp. If you pull it toward you, and you're standing beside the vise, the part may come loose. Be sure to bring your patience with you the first time you work a part held in puppets.

Drawknife and spokeshave work require a sensitivity to grain direction that machine shaping doesn't always require. You must use these tools in the direction of the rising grain. If you try to pull a shaving in the other direction, you're likely to pull out a big unsightly chip.

Once the arm has been shaped using the drawknife, it's time to move on to the more detailed work using chisels, gouges and rasps. When I'm using a rasp, I'm not only clearing away tool marks, I'm also creating lines where the bevel meets the top surface of the arm, where the bevel meets the bottom surface and where the upper and lower bevels meet on the perimeter of the arm. With the rasp, I juggle these lines, moving them up and down a bit so that I get lines that have a consistent sweep as they move around the part. This is, in effect, drawing with the rasp.

After more refining work with the gouge and rasp, I turn to sandpaper. When working the shape with the sandpaper, you don't want to blur the line where the bevel and top come together. Instead, you want to define that line as sharply as possible to add another graphic detail to the shape of the arm.

PHOTO 11 After I've removed the blank from the puppets, I clamp it to my bench and work the nose with a carving gouge.

PHOTO 12 I'm carving the nose of an arm for the walnut splint-back rocker.

PHOTO 13 The refinement of line is further developed using sandpaper.

PHOTO 14 Sometimes, even when you release the pressure of the clamp head, the arm will remain pinned in place. You can release the pressure by tapping on the bottom of the puppet.

PHOTO 15 The original arm was a bandsawn cutout (with the band saw marks removed, of course). My version of that same arm adds bevels which are not only visually interesting but are appealing to the sense of touch by drawing the hand to them.

Bending Chair Parts

All but a handful of the post-and-rung chairs appearing in this book have bent parts. In some cases, only the slats are bent, but most of the chairs in this book have both bent back slats and bent back posts. These parts are bent for two reasons. First, there is an aesthetic appeal to bent parts, which are more interesting to the eye and to the touch. But more important is the comfort bent components can give to a chair. A back post that's been bent back just a few degrees beyond the perpendicular allows a more comfortable sitting posture. And bent back slats that curve

PHOTO 1 This monstrosity is my steamer, with which I plasticize wood parts before bending them. Before placing parts in the steam chamber (the 48" length of PVC), I fill the french fryer with water and bring the water to a boil. I then load my parts into the steam chamber. (They're held above the water level with a cap of hardware cloth screwed to the bottom of the PVC.) I use the traditional wood bender's rule-of-thumb for determining the amount of time a given part requires in the steamer — for every inch of the part's thickness, I steam that part for one hour. This means that a back post with a greatest diameter of $1^3/8$" is steamed for a bit less than $1^1/2$ hours. I make an exception to this rule for chair slats. Although they typically have a thickness of only $1/4$", I steam them for 30 minutes.

in harmony with the human back are more comfortable than unbent slats digging into the middle of the back while leaving either side unsupported.

Also, the No.5 tape-back side chair on page 114 features bent tape bars. These function much like bent back slats to embrace the human back with, in this case, a woven and padded back panel.

Some panel-back chairs, whether woven from Shaker tape or splint, can achieve a similar effect by conforming to the shape of the back pressed against it without the use of any bent parts. The walnut splint-back rocker on page 132 is one such chair.

Wood-bending is an ancient discipline, involving the use of a plasticizing agent, traditionally water or steam, to soften the wood which is then molded to a form. As the wood dries over a period of days, the bend sets. When the material is taken from the bending form, most of the bend remains as a permanent feature of the material.

I practice two kinds of bending in my shop: plasticizing with water and plasticizing with steam. When I'm building Shaker oval boxes, I plasticize the box and lid bands with warm water, but cold water will also work. When I'm bending chair parts, I use steam which, I believe, penetrates more deeply into heavy chair parts and does a better job of making those parts pliable. I know many chairmakers who use boiling water as a plasticizing agent. For example, Charles Harvey, a chairmaker in Berea, Kentucky, boils his chair posts until they sink — they are then ready for bending.

Many years ago when I started building chairs, we didn't have any surplus money in our budget, so I couldn't afford any of the commercially-made steamers which were then being advertised in *Fine Woodworking*, so I looked for a low-cost option.

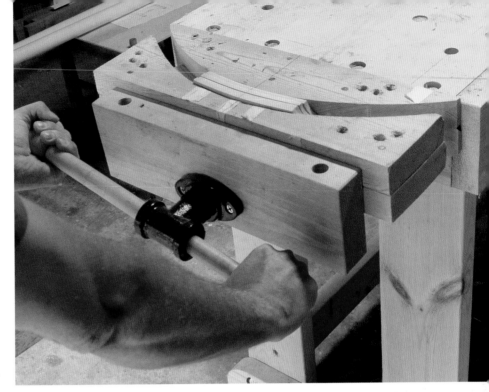

PHOTO 2 My slat-bending forms consist of a male and female half which are sandwiched around the bent slats. In the past, I used to squeeze the sandwiches together in the vise, then hold the sandwiches together with clamps or U-bolts (note the U-bolt holes in the forms). Now I have lots of extra benches with good vises, so I just leave the sandwiches in the vises until the bends are set. I allow a minimun of one week for setting.

My wife had recently purchased a french fryer at a garage sale for next to nothing and I decided it could be my source of steam. For a steam chamber, I bought a 48" length of 4" PVC. I cut a square of metal mesh (also called hardware cloth in this part of the country) and screwed it in place to cover the bottom end of the PVC. It holds the ends of steaming parts above the water in the fryer and allows the steam to wash over them. I then cut a hole in the metal lid of the fryer, inserted the mesh-covered end of the PVC through the hole and fastened it in place with four sheet metal screws inserted through the outside of the PVC just above where it enters the fryer's lid. I later added a cap to the top of the PVC into which I'd drilled a half dozen holes. These holes seem to encourage steam to pass up through the pipe to escape, rather than testing the edges of the fryer's lid. I hold the whole teetering construction upright by spring-clamping

it to a chair back with a short length of splint.

Incredibly, it works. I've been steaming parts in this contraption for almost 30 years.

At one point, I decided my french fryer would someday expire, so I asked my wife to buy a back-up at another garage sale, which she did, but the original fryer works as well today as it did 30 years ago, despite the thick rime of crud baked onto the fryer's inside surface.

Wood bending, like so many chairmaking processes, is not an exact science. Every time you pull parts from the bending forms, you will notice subtle irregularities. Two seemingly identical back posts will emerge from identical bending forms with slightly different bends. (The differences can probably be attributed to differences in the wood of the posts. One absorbs steam more readily than the other, or else one is composed of fibers more resistant to bending than the other.)

PHOTO 3 Four slats can be bent at the same time between the halves of the bending form.

PHOTO 4 Anyone who has bent back posts will tell you that the hardest part of the process is forcing those big thick parts into their bending forms. After years of shop-floor mud-wrestling with back posts, I decided I needed a power assist, so I devised this system to quickly and easily impose a bend. After steaming the back posts for the prescribed length of time, I place them in the bending form with the previously-drilled back-rung mortises facing straight up and the marks for the not-yet-drilled side-rung mortises facing out on both sides of the bending form. (This alignment is critical. If they aren't aligned in this manner, you'll end up with curiously bent and unusable back posts.) I then slide a pair of wood collars over the tops of the posts and slip a big hose clamp over the collars. Next, using a drill with a bit extension (this is necessary to keep the chuck out of the way of the twisting clamp), I power the hose clamp into its tightest position, which forces the desired bend into the posts. The wood collars prevent the metal strapping of the hose clamp from digging into the wood of the posts. (The two clamps hold the bending form in place while I load a pair of posts and impose a bend.)

You'll notice the same thing with slats. A sandwich of four identical slats will emerge from the forms with four slightly different bends.

Bends can change over time, particularly in the case of bends taken from the forms too early. Many years ago, I experimented with taking slats from the forms after only a couple of days, and, while the bends looked good when I assembled the back ladder, a month later two of the slats had straightened out enough to surrender all of their bend.

If you're going to build chairs, you need to understand that the chair-making process is not as precise as, say, marquetry. Bending, for example, simply will not produce perfectly consistent results, no matter how consistently you apply your method. You need to be willing to accept the fact that, even though a set of back slats might have subtle irregularities in their bends you didn't intend, they are perfectly usable.

You need to exercise judgment when you're assessing a set of bends. If they're not good enough, the parts should be returned to the steamer and bent a second time. Be scrupulous about leaving parts in the forms until the bends are set. That means a minimum of one week — two is better.

PHOTO 5 A close-up shows the wood collars and the hose clamp. I use an alternative bending form when I want a more extreme bend in the back posts. You can see that form on page 136 in the chapter about constructing of the Gimson-style arm chair.

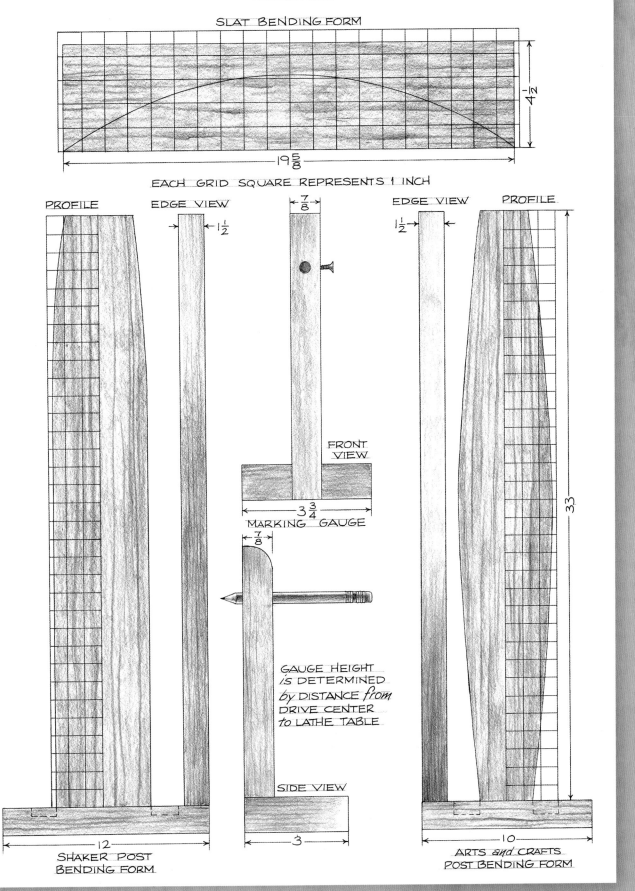

SLAT BENDING FORM

$4\frac{1}{2}$

$19\frac{5}{8}$

EACH GRID SQUARE REPRESENTS 1 INCH

PROFILE

EDGE VIEW

$1\frac{1}{2}$

$\frac{7}{8}$

EDGE VIEW

$1\frac{1}{2}$

PROFILE

FRONT VIEW

$3\frac{3}{4}$

MARKING GAUGE

$\frac{7}{8}$

33

GAUGE HEIGHT
IS DETERMINED
by DISTANCE from
DRIVE CENTER
to LATHE TABLE

SIDE VIEW

12

3

10

SHAKER POST
BENDING FORM

ARTS and CRAFTS
POST BENDING FORM

7

Mortises & Tenons

Post-and-rung chairs are held together with mortise-and-tenon joinery. More specifically, tenons — rectangular or round in cross section — are fit into mortises in the presence of glue, and that glue-assisted union of wood to wood will hold a chair together for decades, despite the daily abuse we give our chairs by shifting our weight from side to side, by scooting the chairs while we sit in them, by leaning back in the chair, lifting the front posts off the floor and teetering on the back posts.

I've been building chairs for 30 years, and I still marvel at the strength of this joinery.

The process of creating mortise-and-tenon joints is incredibly forgiving. I will admit that in my early years as a chairmaker I built some chairs with tenons that were a little less than snuggly fit. But those chairs are still together. They're still providing service in the homes of the men and women who purchased them years ago when my hair was not quite so gray, my hearing not quite so poor and I could read the directions on the back of a soup can without a pair of magnifying glasses.

Simply incredible.

Checking the Evidence

Several times in the last 30 years, I've sliced open old chairs (of my construction) to see how my joinery had fared, and I think my observations of those joints might be worth considering:

1. I used to peg four tenons on every face of every chair using short 1/8"-diameter dowels. For example, I pegged both tenons on the front seat rung and then both tenons on the front bottom rung. This wasn't my idea. There's a long tradition of pegging (or pinning with metal) these tenons, but after I began to slice up my old chairs, I abandoned the pegging process because, when I cut up my pegged chairs, I noticed that every pegged tenon exhibited hairline cracks, something I didn't see in any unpegged tenons.

2. Following the example of Sam Maloof, I used to drive long sheet metal screws through the back post and lengthwise into the arm tenon. Here, too, however, I found splitting when I cut open my chairs. So, despite my enormous respect for Sam Maloof, I've abandoned this practice as well.

In fact, I've abandoned the use of all metal fasteners in chair work because, unlike wood, metal doesn't yield. A screw won't flex when a chair is stressed the way a tenon can flex. A screw retains its stiffness and can, therefore, crack the wood in which it's housed when the chair is stressed.

I now rely on simple unadorned mortise-and-tenon construction to hold my chairs together. (There's one other force at work which I'll explain later.)

3. My round rung tenons have frequently pulled away from one side of the round mortise into which they're placed, probably as a result of tenon shrinkage. This may help to explain why a tenon that isn't tightly fit is apparently as good as one that is tightly fit.

4. Some rectangular-in-cross-section slat tenons seem to have pulled

away from one side of their mortises, but this may be the result of imperfect alignments of those mortises caused by the fact that I chop them by hand, aligning them with my eye.

Beyond these four specific conclusions, the study of my old chairs sug-

gests to me some more generalized observations.

First, the chairmaking process is forgiving. To demonstrate the degree of that forgiveness, I'd like to share the experience of one of my students at the Marc Adams School several years ago.

Making Accurate Mortises

PHOTO 1 Here I'm releasing the pin to adjust the indexing head on my lathe. The indexing head lets me identify any of 36 equally-spaced locations on the piece. If your lathe lacks this feature, you can lock it with a wrap of duct tape that runs around the spindle, then reaches onto the headstock at either end.

PHOTO 2 Once the lathe's rotation is locked, I slide this little marking jig (see page 57 for details) along my lathe table so it leaves a pencil line on the spindle's outside surface. This line is parallel to the spindle's axis of rotation.

On the third day of class, I stopped by his bench to admire his recently assembled back ladder — it was worthy of admiration. The ladder stood square and tall, in one plane when sighted from above. The hand-chopped slat mortises fit each slat snuggly. It was undeniably a good-looking ladder, but I nevertheless had the sense that something about this ladder was wrong. I looked at the ladder and at the rungs he had left on his bench. There were six, the six side rungs he would use to join the front and back ladders. Only they weren't all side rungs. Three looked to be the shorter back rungs that should

have been part of the back ladder I'd been admiring. I pulled out my rule to check the lengths of the rungs he'd used on his back ladder, and yes, he had assembled that ladder with three side rungs at the bottom instead of the three back rungs he should have used.

If you've ever been at the bench assembling a chair, you know how easy it is to make that mistake. Despite differences in length, all the rungs look about the same.

I broke the news to the chairmaker and he was horrified. It was far too late to safely break the glue joints and disassemble the back ladder, and he was convinced his chair was ruined.

I told him not to worry and had him turn three more side rungs. I said the chair would be just fine and no one would notice the error. "Of course, you'll always know," I said. "But no one else will." Some months after he finished the chair and the class, he sent me an e-mail. He thanked me for the class and said the chair was fine — sometimes even he forgot about the extra-long back rungs.

The other observation I made after my study of my sawn-up chairs is that mortise tightness is not as critical as many expect it to be. A joint that fits less-than-perfectly can be a completely successful joint.

Making Accurate Mortises continued

PHOTO 3 Lay the post story stick on the post and transfer the marks to the post. This particular story stick (for the front post of the Union Village rocker), has more information than just the locations of the centers of rung mortises which are indicated on the stick by squared black lines. The stick also indicates the locations of decorative scorings, which are marked on the story stick by squared red lines. As you can see, by the time I was ready to mark rung mortise locations, I had already incised the scorings.

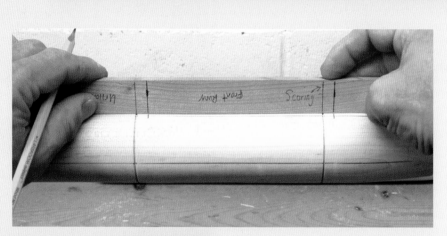

PHOTO 4 Once you've marked your mortises, it's time to use the front-rung-mortise jig (FRMJ) to align the post for the drilling of the front and back rung mortises. (See the measured drawing for this jig on page 67.) I set the drill-press table height until it looks about right. I then test the setup using a piece of scrap post of the correct diameter and check the depth of the mortise with my rule. Usually, this requires three or four adjustments until I get the perfect mortise depth, which is 1" for all $7/8$"-long tenons.

This agrees with a word of caution I usually offer my students about tenon tightness. Some first-timers want every tenon to be just as tight as it can be, thinking that this will produce a better chair. Unfortunately, the reverse is true. It's better for tenons to be a little loose. If all the tenons are profoundly tight, there is no way to assemble a chair. You need to remember that tenons (and mortises) swell as they absorb moisture from the glue, which can make them more difficult to bring together wet than dry, even with the lubricating effect of glue. Plus, tightness accumulates. When you're assembling a back ladder with

six rung tenons and eight slat tenons, you need a bit of wiggle room in each, or the ladder simply will not come together no matter how much you pound on it or how much pressure you apply with pipe clamps.

I recommend this test of tenon tightness: With the post clamped to your bench, insert a rung you believe might be too loose into a mortise. If it goes in easily and the rung stands straight, the tenon is good. If it goes in easily but the rung slouches to one side, the tenon is too loose and should be either repaired or replaced.

I usually replace a rung with a seriously undersized tenon. I find

that easier than fiddling with a repair, but it is possible to make a repair by gluing a planed shaving around the undersized tenon and then re-sizing the tenon.

Mortise & Tenons

My lathe is equipped with an indexing head that allows me to lock the work's rotation in any of 36 equally-spaced locations. (The space between any two of these locations represents 10° of the spindle's circumference.) I do this by releasing a spring-loaded pin into a hole drilled in a metal disk centered on the lathe's axis of rotation. This disk is the lathe's indexing head.

With the lathe rotation locked, I mark a center line along the length of the piece. I use a simple jig shown in Photo 2. Your lathe is probably different than mine, so your marking gauge might be shaped differently as well. All you need is a way to hold the pencil at a height equal to the distance between the lathe's axis of rotation and the bench top so you can slide the tip of the pencil along the spindle's outside surface. Remember that the line on which you'll be marking back rung (and slat) mortises must extend the full length of the back posts. The line marking the side rung and arm mortises need extend only as high on the post as the arm.

As you can see in Photo 3, I've used my marking gauge to make two lines parallel to the spindle's axis of rotation on the spindle's outside surface. The one on which I'm marking is the center line of the front rung mortises. The other line, which can be seen between my hands near the bottom of the spindle, is the line on which I'll mark the centers of the side-rung mortises.

The angular distance between these lines is 80°. Because my lathe's indexing head is calibrated in 10° increments, it's easy for me to mea-

PHOTO 5 I place the post in the FRMJ so that the center line along which I'll be drilling is a distance from the jig's fence that is one half of the post's diameter. In the case of this back post with a diameter of about 1⁷/₈", I rotate this post so that its center line is about ¹⁵/₁₆" from the jig's fence. I then turn the 1¹/₄" drywall screws into the post's end grain to lock it so that it won't rotate when it's passed under the drill bit of the drill press.

sure 80°. I simply count eight stops with the lathe's spring-loaded pin and lock the lathe.

If your lathe lacks an indexing head, you can easily produce an acceptable line placement, using duct tape, to lock the post's position. First I need to convince you that the method I'm going to recommend will work.

When you're making these guidelines along the lengths of your posts' outside surfaces, the only critical aspect of the line is that it be parallel to the part's axis of rotation. That is critical because if you start chopping slat mortises centered on a line that isn't parallel, you'll end up with slats twisting from the posts at all angles.

Fortunately it's easy to make that line parallel with the part's axis of rotation. Once you've locked the rotation, whether it be with a pin in an indexing head or a wrap of duct tape, any line you make while sliding the marking jig along your lathe table will be perfectly parallel with the part's axis of rotation.

The second line, the one that's supposed to be 80° from the first, needs be approximately 80° from the first. Later the side-rung-mortise jig will create the precise distance between the lines. You can rotate the post, make a guess and tape the post in place before sliding the jig along the table to mark the post.

It's easy to make a guess. 80° is a bit less than 90°, which is one-quarter of the distance around the spindle's circumference. Eyeball one-quarter of the distance around the spindle, adjust the rotation to a bit less than that, and you're ready to tape and mark. (I admit that if I were reading this, I might be skeptical. I guarantee that the duct-tape method will work if you proceed the way I suggest.)

The purpose of the front-rung-mortise jig (FRMJ) is to ensure that the center lines of all the rungs on one side of the chair will lay in the same

PHOTO 6 If you're having trouble holding the post in the right position while you turn in the drywall screws, you can clamp it before turning in the screws.

PHOTO 7 Drill the three front-rung mortises.

PHOTO 8 Once the back-rung mortises have been drilled (and the post bent, if necessary), you're ready to chop the slat mortises. Fix the post on your bench top with clamps and U-blocks as shown.

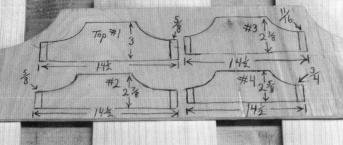

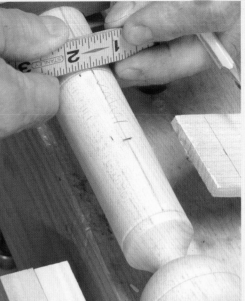

PHOTO 9 On every back slat pattern, I record all the information necessary to install the back slats. Notice that the slats are numbered– #1, #2, #3, #4—with #1 representing the top slat. It's important that you keep them in order because each one will be handled a little differently.

PHOTO 10 I'm laying out the slat mortises on the post. The center line I made on the lathe with my marking jig is the key. This center line passed through the center lines of the back-rung mortises I drilled in this post using the FRMJ and will be used as the *front* edge of each slat mortise.

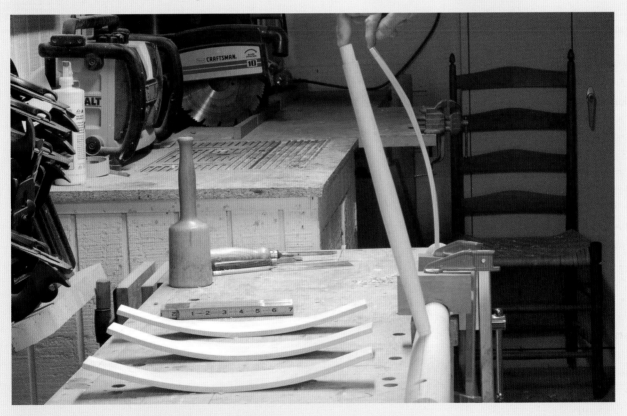

PHOTO 11 Please study this photo before going any farther. As I stated in the caption for Photo 10, because of their bends, the slats don't enter the post in the same alignment as the rungs. They enter behind the center line rather than centered on it, and, they enter at an angle. Note the different rung and slat angles.

The problem when you're chopping slat mortises is that you must do so at an angle that will cause the bent slat to enter one back post in a way that brings the other end of the bent slat into the other back post at the correct angle.

I use one of the back rungs in the bottom back rung mortise as a reference against which I check the progress of each slat mortise. To make the check, I work a slat into a partially completed mortise, then step back and sight the ladder from the bottom of the post. When the angle of my mortise is correct, the slat arcs away from the center line of the rung and then back to it when it reaches the location of the second back post, which, of course, not yet in place.

plane. You could drill these mortises, holding the post from rotating with your hand (and I did for several years), but the human eye isn't capable of picking the absolute center of a pencil line each time you slide the post to a new position along its length. Even a couple of degrees of error in the center line of each rung can create huge problems when you try to force the ladder to lay flat. This jig prevents any rotation.

The first version of the FRMJ was made from a length of 2×4 with a thickness of $1^1/_2$". Because some of the chairs in this book have post diameters greater than $1^1/_2$", I attached some additional thickness so I would have something to measure against when I was aligning posts in the jigs.

Important: Use the FRMJ to drill only the front-rung mortises on the front posts and the back-rung mortises on the back posts. If you make a mistake and use this jig to align the drilling of the side-rung mortises, you'll have to make new posts.

In the case of this particular chair, the slats are all the same length, but many chairs have back slats of varying lengths with the higher slats being wider than those in the middle of the ladder near the seat. Notice that the tenons on each slat are different lengths. The tenons on the two top slats are $5/_8$" long, while the tenon on slat No.3 is $11/_{16}$" and the tenon on slat No.4 is $3/_4$". These tenons lack shoulders. The measurements simply indicate the amount of each slat that will be housed in its mortise.

As I begin to lay out the mortises on the post, I recognize that because the slats are bent, they need to enter the post behind that center line in order to be positioned on a line that will intersect its axis of rotation. My decision to use the rung mortise's center line as the slat mortise's front side is a

PHOTO 12 It's difficult to chop $1/_4$" mortises with a $1/_4$" mortise chisel. While you can drive the $1/_4$" chisel in between the front and back lines of the $1/_4$" mortise, you can't lever chips out. So, I ground down the sides of my mortise chisel so the chisel measures about $1/_{32}$" less than $1/_4$".

PHOTO 13 I nibble a row of chips loose with my mortise chisel.

PHOTO 14 I register the tip of a paring chisel in the scored line that defines each side of the mortise and tap out the chips.

PHOTO 15 I work my way deeper into the mortise, repeating the nibbling process and making frequent checks of the mortise's angle by comparing a partially inserted slat against the reference spindle in the bottom-rung mortise.

PHOTO 16 The completed mortise should be clean all the way around.

PHOTO 17 Ideally, the slat should look like it grew out of the post at that angle.

little arbitrary. It's not a perfect alignment because the amount of bend is variable, but it's a good approximation. With a marking knife, I score the front and back side of each slat mortise. Then I'm ready to start chopping.

When I was hired to write this book, my editors at F+W made it clear that the operative word in the book's description was *simplified*. The goal was to present a method of building chairs that was stripped of complications.

With that in mind, I re-designed both my front-rung-mortise jig (FRMJ) and my side-rung-mortise jig (SRMJ), making each simpler and easier to use.

The FRMJ is straightforward. It's designed to keep the center lines of front-rung mortises in the same plane while mortises are drilled.

The SRMJ is a different animal. To understand how it operates and brings simplicity to the chairmaking process, I need to give you a little background.

A Useful & Deliberate Error

All chair-rung mortises are drilled at compound angles. Take side rungs for example. In one plane, there is the angle that connects the center line of the side rung and the center line of the post to which it will be attached. In another plane, there is the angle that connects the center line of the side rung with the center line of an adjacent front or back rung.

In most chairs, the angle that connects the center line of the side rung and the post is 90°. That is a rarely violated standard. (You can find a discussion of this angle in the Union Village side chair chapter.) But there is considerable variation in the second angle, the one made by connecting the center line of the side rung and the center line of either the back or front rung.

These are the angles you see when you look down on the chair seat from above, the angles that make the seat wider at the front than it is at the back. In some chairs, the angle made by connecting the center line of the side rung and the center line of the back rung is 100°, in others it's 97.5° and in some, like the splint-back bar stool with a square seat, it's 90°.

The angles that connect the center line of the back rung and the center line of the side rungs are about the same for all chairs with non-square seats. In fact, for the purposes of this book, for the jigs that appear in it and for my current approach to chairmaking, I've chosen to treat these angles as if they are the same and use the same SRMJ to create them all.

The slight variation between an angle of say 100° and an angle of 97.5° will be achieved as a result of the lengths of the rungs used to assemble those chair frames.

I'm going to use the same SRMJ to align the chair ladders for the drilling of these different angles. *In other words, I'm going to drill them at the wrong angles and I'm going to do it on purpose.* In this instance, error is a good thing.

As I said earlier, I used to peg four tenons on each face of a chair in order to use this bit of mechanical joinery to reinforce the chemical joinery of glue. My thinking was, if the glue failed at some point down the road, the pegs would keep the chair from falling apart.

When I stopped using the pegs (because they caused cracks in the tenons), I needed a substitute for that bit of mechanical joinery. That's when I decided to introduce error into the alignment of side-rung mortises.

Years ago, when I first began to build post-and-rung chairs and my mortise angles were all over the place, I was struck by how difficult it was to take apart a dry-assembled chair with rung mortises drilled at the wrong angles. Sometimes, I had to whale away at the posts so hard with my rubber-headed mallet that I was sure something was going to break.

I have always suspected that mortise error might be one of the things keeping traditional hand-built chairs together centuries after their construction. There had to have been error in mortise drilling. After all, the craftsmen were — in many cases — eyeballing the alignment of their hand drills. So what keeps those chairs together two centuries after they were built? I'm sure there is more than one factor at work here — shrinkage of a green-post dry tenon for example. I also suspect that unintentional misalignment of mortises is a part of the mix.

The problem I had was how to make deliberate mortise misalignment work in a controlled fashion. I knew from painful experience that the random misalignment that occurs when you don't have any jigs controlling the process simply wouldn't work. You end up with chairs that lean and chairs that can't set four feet on the floor simultaneously.

After a little experimentation, I settled on the introduction of error in the alignment of side-rung mortises. If the error is exactly the same all the way up and down the chair frame, the chair stays square, doesn't lean and keeps all four feet on the floor simultaneously. And, there is no way to spot this deliberate error in the finished chair. It looks just like a chair in which the side-rung mortises have been drilled at the ideal angle.

In the chair in photo 22, the side rungs have been fitted into their mortises in the back ladder, and they've also been fitted into their mortises in the left side of the front ladder. But as you can see, they don't line up right to be fit into their mortises on the right side of the front ladder. To get those side rung tenons into the right front post, you have to apply a little force which places the whole chair frame

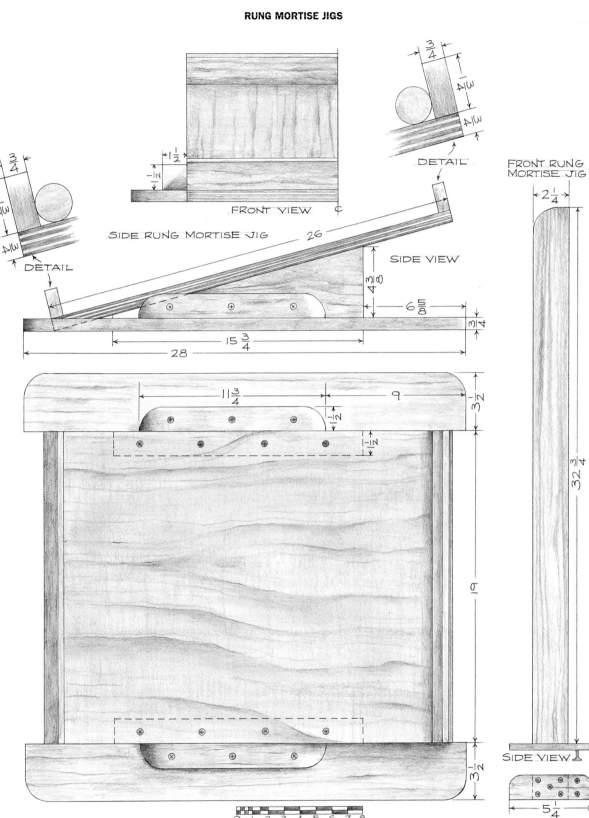

DETAIL

FRONT VIEW

SIDE RUNG MORTISE JIG

DETAIL

SIDE VIEW

FRONT RUNG MORTISE JIG

TOP VIEW

SCALE *in* INCHES

SIDE VIEW

BOTTOM VIEW

under tension. When the tenons have been forced into their mortises, even without glue, you have a chair that won't come apart.

This tension exists not only in the alignment of side rungs and posts, but, throughout the entire chair frame, placing the front and back ladders under stress too.

Using the SRMJ

You can set up the SRMJ (see photo 19) to drill mortises with the post pressed firmly against the fence. You can also use it with the jig set closer to the drill press post so the jig's fence doesn't come into play. There are advantages to each approach. It's reassuring to have the fence set so a hole will be bored in the correct position (at least in regard to the width of the post) when the post is crowded up against it, but it takes more fussing with the jig to get it clamped to the drill press table this way. Sometimes I clamp the jig in an approximately correct position and then drill the mortises while I'm holding the ladder in position with my off hand. Remember: It's the angle of the table, not the fence, that provides the necessary alignment.

In photo 21, note the plywood cleats under the posts. While these wouldn't be necessary on a chair like the walnut splint-back rocker on page 132, they are necessary here because without them, the bend in the slats would cause the middle of the slat to lift the ladder up from a secure position on the jig. In the case of a chair with even more curve in the slats, it might be necessary to add a double-thickness of plywood cleats.

PHOTO 18 Before settling on the jig you see here, I experimented with several versions, each imposing different degrees of error. One jig resulted in much less error than you see in chairs produced with this jig, so little, in fact, that I gained too little tension to keep dry chairs together. And another was so close to 90° that I couldn't get the chair together without whipping them into submission. The jig you see here is a compromise.

My decision to deliberately introduce a substantial error into the drilling of side-rung mortises not only provides my chairs with a mechanical resistance to disassembly, but it also means there is no reason to create different side-rung jigs for each subtly different set of side-rung angles. The result is a non-adjustable, one-size-fits-all side-rung-mortise jig, which corresponds nicely with my assignment for this book — keep things simple.

The jig is designed to be used in two different alignments. With the jig sloping down toward the drill press operator, the jig is aligned for drilling side-rung mortises in the back ladder. When it is rotated 180° and used with the jig sloping away from the operator, as it is shown here, it's aligned for drilling side-rung mortises in front ladders

PHOTO 19 I prepare for the drilling process by setting the drill-press table height. When the bit is fully lowered, it drills a 1" deep hole into the center of the post.

PHOTO 20 With the ladder crowded against the fence, I slide it to the left and right in order to properly locate the mortises along the length of the post.

PHOTO 21 I rotate the jig 180° and set it up to drill mortises in the back posts. This requires me to set the depth of cut using a piece of scrap post of the correct diameter.

PHOTO 22 Where the side rungs approach the front post on the right, you can see the error the SRMJ deliberately introduces into mortise placement. This error keeps the chair together even in the event of glue failure.

8

Assembling Chairs

Apost-and-rung chair is assembled in stages. The first stage is the assembly of the front and back ladders once all their mortises have been formed.

Without question, the back ladder is the most difficult part of the chair to assemble because there are so many parts (2-5 slats and 2-3 rungs with each part having two tenons that must be fit into two mortises) that have to come together just right. I recommend you use a helper for the assembly of back ladders, but, having said that, I admit I always work alone.

Working alone, preparation is extremely important. Before adding glue to anything, I test fit all tenons into their mortises and make sure that all fit easily, because a tenon that's snug when you're fitting that single tenon into its single mortise can become a nightmare when that tenon is one of 14-16 you're trying to fit simultaneously. (Remember: Tightness accumulates.)

Photo 1 shows things almost ready to go, but, looking at the photo, I can see I forgot one thing. I don't yet have my pipe clamp out that I use to drive tenons into their mortises. The clamp is important because once you've got a tenon started into its mortise, you can't drive it home with a mal-

PHOTO 1 Because I work alone, I take the time to prepare everything before attempting an assembly this complicated. I have clamped one back post — mortises-up — to the top of my bench. I've aligned all the rungs and slats in the correct positions. The second back post is nearby. I've filled a paper cup with glue and placed a couple of glue spreaders beside it. I have a bucket of water on the floor and a rag on the bench so I can wash away glue squeeze out. The one thing I've forgotten is a pipe clamp which is important because once you've got a tenon started into its mortise, you can't drive it home with a mallet without breaking something. You need to apply slow steady pressure to force it home.

let without breaking something. You need to apply slow steady pressure to force it home. Plus, slat tenons will often hang up on the sides of their mortises. The cure for this problem is to place a pipe clamp across the front side of the ladder at the same height as the stuck slat. Then draw up the pipe clamp. If the stuck tenons don't unstick, grab the top of the slat with your fingers and the pipe of the clamp with your thumbs and squeeze. The slat will flex, and the tenons will pop into their mortises.

After the back is assembled and the glue is still wet, you should check the back for twist as shown in Photo 2. Any error can be corrected by racking the ladder. You should also check the ladder for squareness. I use a framing square with one leg on a bench top and the other alongside a post. In the case of front ladders, both posts should be perpendicular to the

PHOTO 2 This is the assembled ladder after I've juggled, tugged and muscled each tenon into its mortise. Frequently, a newly assembled back ladder will exhibit some twist which you can see by sighting it from above. When you see this, lock the bottoms of the ladder between your feet as I'm doing here. Then twist the ladder one way or the other to remove the twist.

PHOTO 3 Glue can hide in many places on a chair. To make sure all the excess glue is eliminated, I use a toothbrush and water to brush away glue at the intersections of post and slats or post and rungs.

bench top, but in the case of a back ladder that might spread as it rises from the floor, what you're looking for is an equal amount of error on either side, making corrections by racking the ladder.

While it doesn't matter so much in the case of a chair that's going to be painted, every speck of glue must be washed away from a chair that will be given a natural finish (Photo 3). Don't shirk this process because, if you do,

you will regret it when you apply that first coat of finish and every glue spot you couldn't see when you were sanding suddenly starts flashing like a neon sign.

Even with all of your preparation work in order, the assembly process can still be hectic. Even when you think you've checked everything, you can still miss a detail like the slat in Photo 4 which I didn't seat as deeply as I should have.

After the glue holding the front and back ladders together has cured, the frame is assembled by joining the front and back ladders with the six side rungs (Photos 5 & 6).

Next, if the chair you're building has arms, turn your attention to that task. With the chair shown in Photo 7, I'm using a wedged through tenon at the top of each front post to lock the arms in place. These wedges need to be aligned so that their width is perpendicular to the grain directions

PHOTO 4 Things don't always come together quite the way you want them to. This reference line — which should be just a bit outside of the post — is at least ⅛" from the post. This means that I wasn't able to properly center this slat during assembly. I must have had the slat pushed all the way to the bottom of the mortise in the other post. (I cut the mortises a bit deeper than necessary to give me some wiggle room at assembly.) In the case of this tenon on this slat, all the wiggle room ended up on one side. It's unfortunate but certainly not significant.

PHOTO 5 Here's another look at the deliberate error in side-rung angle I discussed in the mortising chapter.

PHOTO 6 I'm using a pipe clamp to squeeze the tenons home. The little twist you see in the back ladder is the result of as-yet-unseated side rung tenons.

PHOTO 7 Align both wedge notches at the same time so that they lay along one continuous line across the width of the chair. Using a straight edge as a guide, I'm drawing lines in the middle of the top of each through tenon.

of the parts in which the tenons are housed — in this case the arms. A straight edge helps with the alignment of the two saw cuts that will create space for the wedge as shown in photos 7 & 8. Photos 9-12 demonstrate installation of the arms and the decorative (and useful!) wedges.

If you're building a rocking chair, there are additional assembly steps. To install the rockers on the chair shown, you need to cut notches in the posts to accept the rockers.

As you look at the step shown in Photo 13, please note that the notches are not the same depth on the front and back posts. In fact, they aren't the same depth on the front and back of the same post. Take measurements from the drawing of your rocking chair and mark the front and back depth on each post. Even then, you may need to do some juggling to get the rockers to fit tightly at the front and back of each post.

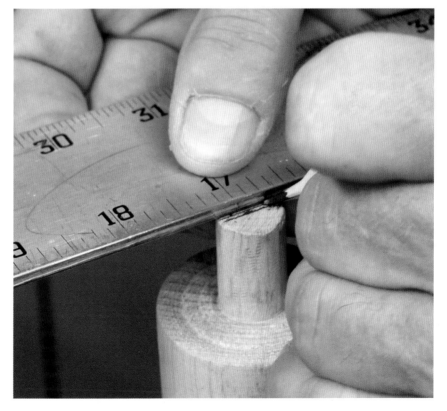

PHOTO 8 This detail shows the two pencil lines I've made at the top of each post. I'll saw down between these lines and remove a slender wedge of maple which I'll later replace with a darker wedge of cherry after the arm has been installed.

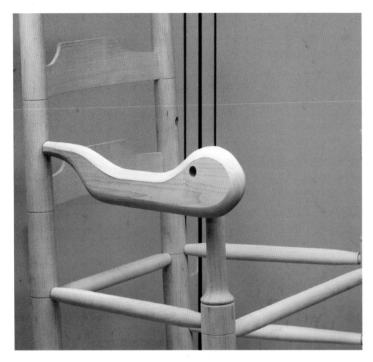

PHOTO 9 To install an arm, I first stand it on its edge and work the tenon into its mortise in the back post. I then roll the arm up over the tenon at the top of the front post.

PHOTO 10 I'm cutting wedges from a bit of scrap cherry.

The rocker notches for the two posts that will be joined by a single rocker (on one side of the chair) must be laid out simultaneously in order for the rocker to simultaneously fit both notches. And you can't mark them together with a conventional straightedge because it won't sit squarely on the ends of the two posts. I use custom-made straightedges (shown in photo 13) with shallow bird's mouths cut in their bottoms to accept the posts.

With the rocker notch locations determined, photos 14 and 15 show the steps to mark and create the notches. The rockers are fit, glued and pinned in place.

PHOTO 11 After the wedges are cut and fit, I apply glue to the tenon on the arm and its mortise and the tenon on the post and its mortise. Then I install the arm. The last thing I do is glue and tap the wedge in place.

PHOTO 12 I saw away any surplus length of the wedge and tenon, then plane them flat.

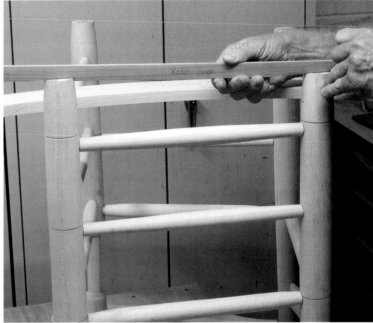

PHOTO 13 To align the two notches for a rocker, I use custom-made straightedges with shallow bird's mouths cut into their bottoms to accept the posts. This allows me to get my straightedge right down on the ends of the posts which enables me to make accurate marks.

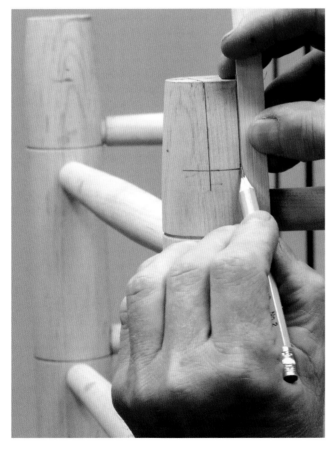

PHOTO 14 I use a flexible straight edge to establish lines for the sides of each notch.

PHOTO 15 I remove the waste from the notch by drilling a hole through the post at the base of the notch. Then I break the waste into thin chunks with a chisel. I then fit the rocker and fasten it in place with dowels that run through the posts and the rocker.

Finishing Chairs

In October of 2003, I was diagnosed with Stage 4 Non-Hodgkins lymphoma and given only a slight chance of surviving the disease. But I was lucky, although at the time that was hard to see. Thanks to the diligence of my family, I managed to get into a clinical trial at the James Cancer Hospital in Columbus, Ohio. It was a course of treatment that required me to admit myself to the James every two weeks for five days of continuous infusion chemotherapy. It was a brutal experience that left me staggered and stumbling at the end of each five-day session, but it worked. Despite the dozens of tumors manifested by my cancer, I'm still alive, and my current prognosis is good.

My survival wasn't a miracle, but it was as close as I ever hope to get to one.

I mention my cancer because, according to my oncologist, my disease was probably the result of decades of daily and irresponsibly intimate exposure to various finishing materials. For 40 years, I ended each day in the shop with a finishing session during which I applied a first, second or third coat to whatever piece was ready for finishing. I did this without protection: no gloves, no long-sleeved shirt, no respirator (unless I was spraying), and, perhaps worst of all, I used liberal amounts of mineral

This is what I consider the bare minimum for working safely with most woodworking finishes: *Disposable brushes* reduce any clean-up exposure to solvent, the *respirator* (whether spraying a finish or not) keeps much of the airborne concern at bay and the *rubber gloves* and a *long-sleeved shirt* keep the finish away from your skin. (These gloves are due for replacement.)

spirits to wash away whatever finish had gotten onto my hands and arms.

I don't blame the finish manufacturers for my disease. There were warnings on the cans and I ignored them. Plus, I think my disease was not solely a result of my irresponsible use of finishing products. I have friends who have done the same thing I did without getting cancer. I think, in my case, the development of my disease was helped along by a genetic predisposition to lymphoma.

The blame is mine entirely, and I haven't wasted a minute trying to shift the responsibility onto someone else's shoulders. Instead, I've tried to learn from my mistakes.

Unfortunately, you can't build furniture without making use of some of the products that may have con-

tributed to my cancer, so I continue to use them — but now I use them responsibly.

Here are my current rules for the use of finishing materials:

1. With the exception of brushes used for water-based paints, I now use disposable brushes. Cleaning my brushes at the end of a finishing session was the context for much of my exposure to mineral spirits.

2. When I apply potentially dangerous finishing materials, I wear a respirator, protective gloves and a long-sleeved shirt.

3. When I apply these materials, I do it either in a different room other than the one in which I'm working or in my bench room at the end of the day so that the air has time to clear before I return to work in that room.

Wipe-off Finishes

Twenty-five years ago, when I discovered the Sam Maloof finishing mixture of equal parts polyurethane, boiled linseed oil and mineral spirits, my finishing practices were revolutionized. Finally, I could eliminate the problems of dust motes settling on surfaces to which I had applied spray-on or brush-on finishes. This is a problem that had plagued my work since I took my first fumbling steps in the workshop late in the 1960s.

I could apply a coat of the Maloof mixture, wipe it off, and then run a table saw in the same room and no dust would stick to the newly finished surface.

For the next 15 years, I applied this finish with consistently good results. Then, maybe ten years ago, I teamed up with a friend to build a set of dining room furniture. He was building a curly maple huntboard and dining table, and I was building the eight curly maple chairs that would sit at that table. I wanted our finishes to have the same look, so I asked my friend what he was going to apply. Waterlox, he said. So I tried this tung-oil product and liked it very much. For the next eight years, that was my primary finish. Like the Maloof mixture, it was a wipe-on, wipe-off product that was immune to dust incursions, and it had the advantage of coming to me ready to use. I didn't have to keep three products on hand and then mix them when I was ready to finish.

Although I like working with Waterlox, it does have one shortcoming: The product sometimes solidifies after even brief exposure to the air, so if you use only a third of a can during one finishing session and then two weeks later you reach for that can to use the remaining two thirds, the remaining finish is likely to have congealed into a solid lump at the bottom of the can. This led me to my next finishing product.

One day, when I discovered that the only can of Waterlox in my shop had solidified, I picked up a can of Minwax Wipe-On Polyurethane at Lowe's and found that it had nearly the same working properties as Waterlox. Two coats — sometimes three — built up a finish that looked good to the eye and felt good under the hand.

More recently, I've been using Gel Topcoat produced by General Finishes and available from Woodcraft, with the same result. Two or three coats gives me a nicely filled and leveled surface, one that has a satisfyingly satiny luster and a silky feel.

Although I recommend all the products I've mentioned here, Gel Topcoat has one appealing characteristic not shared by the others:

I use Waterlox, Minwax Wipe-On Poly and General Gel Coat interchangeably. All produce good results.

Because it's a gel and not a liquid, it doesn't seep into tiny gaps in joints to later bleed out as the finish dries.

Liquid products — like Minwax Wipe-On Poly and Waterlox — penetrate into the tiniest gaps in joinery, and then, over a period of hours, as the finish cures, this excess finish seeps out, making it necessary to re-wipe those areas in order to avoid an unsightly build up. This is sometimes a problem with rocker notches. Unless you're scrupulous with your wiping in that area, you might end up with shiny trails on the rockers below the notches. Gel Topcoat doesn't penetrate. Because of its gelatinous consistency, it stays on the surface where I want it to stay.

I should mention that I've grouped these products in the same arbitrary category, not because they share any

chemistry. I group them together based on style of application. All these products are applied in the same way, and all produce consistently appealing finishes, so in my mind, they all belong in the same category. I apologize to any chemists who might be reading this.

Constructing a Finish

There are only two secrets to the construction of a good wipe on/wipe off finish. One is careful surface preparation — sanding. The other is a careful wiping technique.

When I talk about sanding, I'm talking about hand sanding, a category that includes lathe sanding, as well as the hand sanding you do on your bench once the chair's turned parts have been assembled.

A smoothing plane removes all the ridges left behind by the planer. It's much easier to remove the ridges with a plane than with sandpaper.

Step #1 When slat and rocker and arm stock comes out of your thickness planer, it has a gently rippled surface. The height of those ripples is determined by the speed at which work is fed past the knives and the depth of cut those knives are set to take. The surface will also likely have some areas of tearout. A slow feed rate and a shallow depth of cut will minimize but not eliminate these problems. All stock exiting a thickness planer will have ripples and tearout, even if those features are so faint they can be seen only under magnification.

The first step in creating a good finish is the removal of the ripples and the tearout. The weapon of choice for this task is a good-quality, well-tuned smoothing plane with a sharp iron and a tight mouth.

With your smoothing plane, take light passes, working in the direction of the rising grain. The object here is to remove a consistently thin skin of wood, a skin that contains the ripples and the tearout. If the plane is well set up, it should do this, leaving behind a minimum of tearout and no ripples.

A scraper is a good alternative for figured stock.

Step #2 If you don't have a good smoothing plane, move directly from the planer to sanding (by hand, of course). The use of a mediocre smoothing plane can actually create more problems than it solves, by tearing out otherwise reasonably clean surfaces.

Most good craftsmen sand their work through a succession of grits, starting with relatively coarse paper which removes stock quickly (but leaves behind deep scratches) and following that with progressively finer grits, each of which removes the scratches left by the previous grit. You

Scraping is another option for removing planing ridges. The tool shown above is a card scraper, used primarily with flat surfaces.

I a surface exhibits deep scratches or plane tearout, you may want to begin your sanding with 400-grit sandpaper. In most situations, however, you can use 150 as your first grit, then switching to 220 and 320. Some craftsmen stop there. For pieces that will be given a natural finish, I recommend going one step further to 400 grit.

could theoretically start with the fine grit with which you intend to finish, but it would take several lifetimes to smooth a rocking chair if you went directly from the planer to, say, 320-grit sandpaper.

The specific grits in that succession will vary from craftsman to craftsman. For instance, I begin with 150-grit paper and finish with 400-grit paper, stopping at 220 and 320 along the way. But some craftsmen will start with 120 and move to 180 and 220 before they stop at 320.

Step #3   Following the directions on the can, apply a coat of wipe on/wipe-off finish. Then wipe it off.

The removal wipe is important. You should wipe thoroughly but not scrub. Leave a film only a few molecules thick. (I know what you're thinking. I've never actually counted molecules. But I think it's helpful to think of the wiped finish in this way.) Any areas on which there is extra finish will dry rough and pebbly. But you don't want to scrub the surface dry because, if you do, there won't be enough finish left to fill the surface, and an unfilled

surface won't have the leveled sheen that is the hallmark of a good finish.

The wipe should be done with a relatively absorbent and relatively lint-free fabric. I find old T-shirts are just about perfect. White T-shirts are best because they don't contain any dyes, but any T-shirt without screen-printed graphics will work. (You can't use fabric with screen-printed graphics because the solvents in the wipe-off finishes will dissolve the paint in the graphics, leaving colored smears on the work you're wiping.) If you're not sure about the dye in your T-shirt fabric, experiment on scrap before using it on the piece you're finishing.

Allow the finish to dry overnight. Then sand lightly with 400-grit paper to remove any grain raised by the first coat of finish. Sand only long enough to smooth the surface. You should be able to tame the raised grain on a chair in less than an hour. Test the smoothness with your fingers.

Wipe off the sanding dust. Then apply a second coat of wipe-off finish using the same method you used for the first. This second coat should dry

smooth because you sanded away the raised grain before applying this second coat. If it doesn't dry smooth, re-sand with 400-grit paper and apply a third coat of wipe-off finish.

Step #4   When a situation calls for a glossy sheen or the tactile quality of wax, I will top off my finish with a coat of good paste wax. I use a Minwax product called Finishing Wax with very good results, although contrary to what some craftsmen think, those very good results are not easily achieved.

It's pretty tricky to get a good wax spread. Areas on which there isn't enough wax won't buff out to a sheen no matter how hard you rub, and areas in which there is too much wax won't buff out properly either. These areas with too much wax will always remain a little pebbly. Only those areas on which you've applied a consistently thin layer of wax will buff out to the proper sheen.

And it can be very difficult to properly apply that consistently thin coat of wax on the complicated surfaces of a chair.

A carefully prepared surface can result in a finish that reveals unexpected depth in the materials to which a finish has been applied.

Most finishers apply wax using several layers of cheesecloth in which they've nested a ball of wax. They rub the cheesecloth over the surface to be waxed, and the wax penetrates through the openings in the cheese-cloth leaving behind, theoretically, an even layer of wax. I've tried this method, but I'm more comfortable with my own method.

I simply wad up a bunch of lint-free fabric, once again T-shirt material is my favorite, dab it into the wax until the bottom of the wad is covered in a layer of wax — think a thin spread of margarine on a slice of toast — and wipe the wax onto the surface.

Before I allow the wax to dry, I hold up the surface to a good side light to check my coverage. If I don't have the consistently thin layer I want, I load up my fabric wad and re-wax. (The solvents in the wax will re-liquify any wax that might have dried.)

After the wax has dried for about 30 minutes, I use a ball of clean T-shirt

fabric and some vigorous rubbing to buff it out to the required sheen.

I can get a finish to look the way I want it to look without wax, but I can't get it to feel the way I want it

to feel without wax, and because of their intimate contact with the human body, chairs will be touched, and the touchers should be rewarded with a pleasurable tactile experience.

I apply paste wax with a ball of clean T-shirt fabric on which I've spread a thin layer of wax.

81

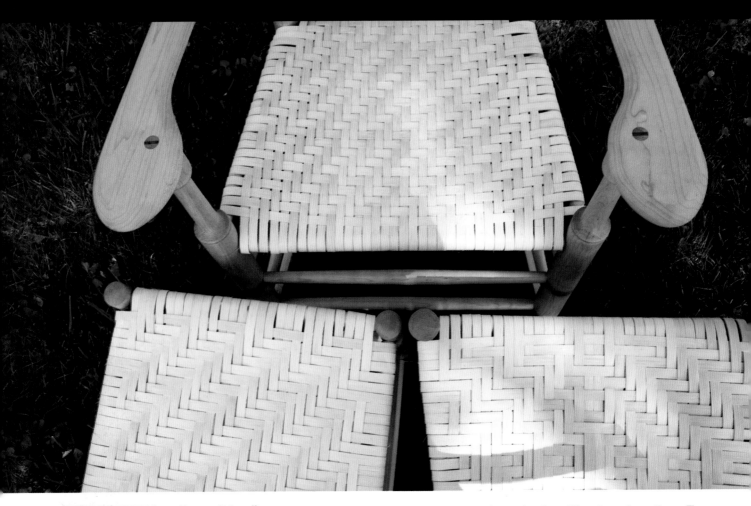

Weaving Splint Seats

The splint traditionally used for American chair seating is a product of ash, white oak or hickory trees. To produce it, green logs are barked and scored, then beaten with a maul, which causes the scored strips to loosen, enabling them to be pulled from the surface of the log. It's good seating material,

The chairs in this book having splint seats are done using three different weaving patterns. The Union Village rocker at the top has a herringbone pattern in which the weaver passes over two warp strands, then under two. The seat of the stool at the bottom left is also done in a herringbone pattern, but in the case of this seat the weaver passes over three warp strands, then under three. The seat of the side chair at the lower left is executed in a diamond pattern.

but it's very expensive to buy (when you can find it) and time- and labor-intensive to prepare if you choose to harvest your own. The Caning Shop in Berkeley, California (800-544-3373) is currently offering hand-pounded

ash splint in 200-foot coils for $150. That 200-foot coil would be enough to seat any chair in this book, but there wouldn't be much left over.

Or, you can buy enough rattan splint to seat the same chair for less than $10, which is what I do. In fact, I purchase my splint from Connecticut Cane and Reed (800-227-8498) in 25-hank lots for a bit over $5 a hank.

The rattan palm from Southeast Asia is not a palm tree. It's a palm vine which clings to and climbs over other forest vegetation, with stems sometimes as thick as a man's arm, reaching a length of over 200 feet. The glossy outer peel of the rattan stems is passed under a roller with knives that divide it into strips of varying widths. This produces the glossy-on-one-side material with which caned seats are woven. The pith, the dense inner core of the rattan stem, is likewise split into strips of varying widths, some of which are sold as a substitute for traditional ash splint. This is the splint, sometimes called flat reed, that I use in seating most of the chairs I build.

Splint is sold on one-pound coils, sometimes called hanks. A seat for a Mt. Lebanon No.5 or a No.6 chair will take a hank and a half. If you're doing the seat and back for the walnut splint-back chair appearing on page 132, you should need a bit less than three hanks.

Weaving Splint

As it comes to you from your supplier, splint will be stiff and difficult to handle, but if you soak it in a tub of warm water for about an hour, it will be pliable enough to weave easily.

Before you start the weaving process, hold a piece of splint up to your eyes and bend it. Then flip it over and bend it the other way. You'll notice that one side of each strand is a bit rougher and has more loose fibers lifting from it when you bend the strand. The other side of the strand is smoother with fewer fibers lifting from it. Every strand you apply to your seat should be applied so that the loose fibers are down and the smoother surface up.

But I warn you. Sometimes the difference between one side and the

PHOTO 1 This is the tool kit the weaving process requires. I'll explain the use of each one as we go.

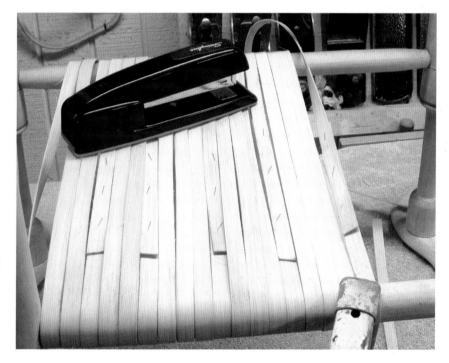

PHOTO 2 The starting end of the first warp strand is taped to the side rung as indicated on the left side of this photo. (You get a better look at this taped strand on a different chair in Photo 9) The warp then continues up under the front rung, over it, then back around the back rung and so on. To splice on a new warp strand, invert the chair, lap 6" of the lead end of a new strand over the final 6" of the old strand and fasten them together with three staples from a conventional office stapler. All warp splices should be on the bottom of the chair.

other is very slight. There have been many occasions when I've pulled out a partially woven strand convinced I had it the wrong side up, and then, after I had re-woven it into the seat with the other side up, I decided that I'd been right in the first place. Fortunately, there are no dire consequences for having a strand woven upside down. The only consequence is that you have more hair to trim from the finished seat.

Before you can apply any splint, you must first establish a rectangle in the center of the chair's seat. That rectangle should be as wide as the distance between the back posts and approximately square at each corner.

You can create the rectangle in two ways.

Method one: lay a framing square just inside the back post, with one leg parallel to the back seat rung and the other leg reaching forward to cross the front seat rung. Make a mark where the forward leg of the square crosses the front seat rung, flip the square over and repeat the process on the inside of the other back post.

Method two: measure the length of the back seat rung between the back

PHOTO 3 Continue wrapping the warp until you've filled the central rectangle of the seat. The final warp strand should pass over the back rung, then under, to the inside of the side rung where it will be taped as you see here. Alternatively, if the spacing works better, you can wrap the last strip of the warp for this central rectangle over the front rung and underneath to the inside of the side seat rung.

posts. Mark this length on the front seat rung, centering it between the front posts.

The interior of this rectangle is the first section you'll weave. Photo 2 shows the bottom side of the rectangle beginning to emerge. Photo

9 shows the emerging rectangle on another chair, this time from the top.

A chair seat weave consists of two elements. The warp is the pattern of strands that runs between the front and back rungs. The weave is the pattern of strands woven perpendicular

PHOTO 4 The first weaver fills the space between the posts on the top of the seat. The strand should go over two and under two as shown for the particular pattern. Tuck both ends under.

PHOTO 5 Start the first long weaver on the bottom of the seat, using the over two and under two pattern.

PHOTO 6 Bring the weaver up around the side rung and work it into the warp, using the over two and under two pattern. Start this second weaver one warp strand back from where the fill weaver entered.

PHOTO 7 Although I splice weavers on both the top and bottom surfaces of chairs, most chairmakers make splices only on the bottom. To make a splice, simply lap the first 6-8" of the new weaver over the last 6-8" of the old weaver. No stapling is required because the tightness of the weave holds the splice together

PHOTO 8 Gusset strips fill the triangular sections of the seat warp on both sides of the seat's central rectangle. When you've finished weaving about half of the seat's central rectangle, begin working these gusset strips into the weave using the same over two/under two pattern, staggering their entry points one strand from the adjacent warp strand. Wrap them over the front rung. Then weave them into the weave on the bottom side of the seat. Tuck the ends under. A butter knife will help you feed these strips into the weave.

PHOTO 9 When you're installing the warp, a spring clamp will hold the tension in the existing warp while you join on a new section.

to the warp. You begin with the warp. Follow photos 2 and 3 through the warp steps, then follow photos 4-7 to work through the weave steps.

The step shown in Photo 6 is tricky. You may struggle with this technique, so take a few moments to study the pattern in the finished seat shown in photo 13 before you begin. Notice that each new strand of weaver begins its entrance into the warp one warp strand back from the point of entrance of the previous weaver strand.

If you make a mistake with your weavers (and you will), nothing is lost. Simply pull out weavers until you reach the mistake. Then re-weave. Also, an occasional weaving mistake is a cosmetic issue only. If, after you've finished the seat, you find a weaving mistake in the first few rows of weavers, it isn't structurally necessary to unweave the whole seat and start again.

The chair seat needs a finish as well. I always apply one more coat of finish to the chair's wood surfaces after weaving the seat because splint weaving can scuff up a finish. I then apply the same finish to the splint that I apply to the wood of the chair. Some finish is necessary in order to keep the splint washable.

Splint will take paint. I have also created patterns by using aniline dye to color some strands of splint before weaving a seat.

You can remove the warp-splice staples on the back of splint-back chairs when you're done because the tightness of the weave will hold the splices tight. You may also remove the staples on the bottom of the seat.

PHOTO 10 I use two different herringbone patterns. The one illustrated in Photos 1-8 is an over two/under two pattern. The one I'm weaving here is an over three/under three pattern. The weaving method is the same except for the count. Both patterns produce good seats, although the over two/under two pattern is noticeably more difficult to weave.

PHOTO 11 A pair of needle-nosed pliers will make it easier to pull the last weavers through the by-now-very-tight warp.

PHOTO 12 This is a finished seat woven with the over three/under three pattern.

PHOTO 13 This is a finished seat with the over two/under two pattern.

PHOTO 14 You can also create geometric shapes with your weavers like the diamond pattern shown here.

11

Weaving Shaker-Tape Seats

In the middle of the nine-teenth century, Shaker crafts-men began using a new material to seat their chairs: the fabric webbing we now refer to as Shaker tape. In those early years, the tape was com-posed primarily of wool fibers, but the tape available today is 100% cotton.

Shaker tape offers several advan-tages over splint. First, the tape is available in a variety of attractive colors. And, a seat composed of 1" tape can be woven in a fraction of the time that seat will require if it is to be woven with splint. But there are disadvantages as well. Shaker tape is much more expensive than splint, and the colors are notorious for fading when used on a chair that's exposed to strong natural light. That said, if the chair is kept in a normal indoor envi-ronment, out of direct sunlight, there is no reason to expect its color to fade any more quickly than the color of upholstered furniture.

I used to buy my tape from Connecticut Cane and Reed, but they stopped handling the product several years ago. I have recently been buying my tape from The Country Seat, Inc. (610-756-6124) and I've been pleased with the quality of their product.

Traditionally, the weaving of a Shaker-tape seat requires some skill with a needle and thread, which I utterly lack. For years, I struggled to attach gusset strips to the warp with stitches, and while I did eventually finish those chairs, I took no pleasure in the work. As a result, I developed a non-traditional way of weaving tape seats, one that doesn't require any sewing. I mention this because, if you want to learn how to weave tape the way the Shakers did, you need to go to another source. But if you're as ham-fisted as I am with sewing tools, you may find my method worth your consideration.

Getting Started

The first step in any kind of seat weaving is creating a central rectangle within the space enclosed in the chair's four seat rungs. That rectangle should be as wide as the distance between the back posts and approximately square at each corner. You can create the rectangle in two ways.

You can lay a framing square just inside the back post with one leg of the square parallel to the back seat rung and the other leg reaching forward to cross the front seat rung. Make a mark then where the forward leg of the square crosses the front seat rung, flip the square over and repeat the process on the inside of the other back post.

Another method used to define the central rectangle is shown in Photo 2, using the back seat rung to determine the rectangle.

Before I start weaving, I cut off enough length of both the warp and weave material to do the entire central rectangle. (The warp is the collection of strips passing over and around the front and back seat rungs and the weave is the collection of strips woven into the warp passing over and around the side seat rungs.) To calculate the amount of warp I need, I determine the number of 1"-wide strips of tape that will be required to cover the back seat rung and multiply that number by twice the distance

PHOTO 1 These are the tools and supplies you need to weave tape seats. I'll explain the use of each one as we go.

PHOTO 2 To create the seat's central rectangle, you can measure the length of the back seat rung between the back posts. Subtract that length from the length of the front seat rung between the front posts. Then make a pair of marks on the front seat rung that is inside each front post a distance equal to half the difference between the lengths of the two seat rungs. Because the rungs on this chair are painted black, I used a pink pencil to mark the front corners of the seat's central rectangle on the front seat rung.

PHOTO 3 To start the weaving process, I fasten the loose end of my warp material to the bottom of the back seat rung just inside one of the back posts using a pair of $^1/_4$" staples.

between the front and back seat rungs. It's twice the distance because the warp runs on both the top and bottom of the seat. I then add in a little extra length, cut that much from the roll, and with it, create a smaller roll, which is easier to handle than the 75-yard roll that I purchased from my supplier. I perform a similar calculation to determine the length of the weave material.

Photos 4 and 5 walk you through the rest of the warp weaving steps. Photo 6 shows the process of adding padding to the seat, which helps to maintain a tight appearing seat.

Photos 7-12 explain the weaving steps and a tool that I find indispensable in this step.

After you've finished weaving the seat, lightly sand the chair's wooden frame, and careful add another coat of finish (in this case paint) to remove any scuffings left by the seat weaving process.

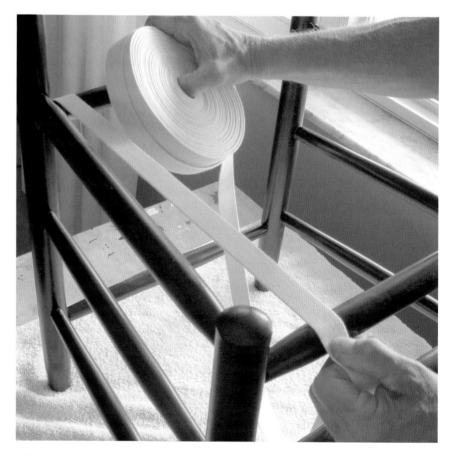

PHOTO 4 I then begin to wrap the warp material over and around the front and back seat rungs, keeping the material inside the marks I made on the front seat rung to establish the limits of the seat's central rectangle.

PHOTO 5 When I've filled the central rectangle, I cut off the surplus length of the warp and staple that end to the bottom of the front seat rung using two $1/4$" staples.

PHOTO 6 I then slip the seat's stuffing into place between the layers of the warp. I prefer 1"-thick foam over the loose stuffing I'm using here because I think it holds its shape better, but the local fabric shop was out of foam. I've used this loose stuffing before with good results. The purpose of the stuffing is to help the seat maintain its taut appearance and to improve its comfort.

PHOTO 7 It's a little hard to see, but what I'm doing here is attaching the end of the wine-colored weaver to the bottom of the side seat rung just ahead of the back post using two $1/4$" staples.

PHOTO 8 I then bring the tape up over the side seat rung and begin to weave the seat by passing the coil alternately over and under the warp strands on the top of the seat. I repeat the process on the bottom of the seat.

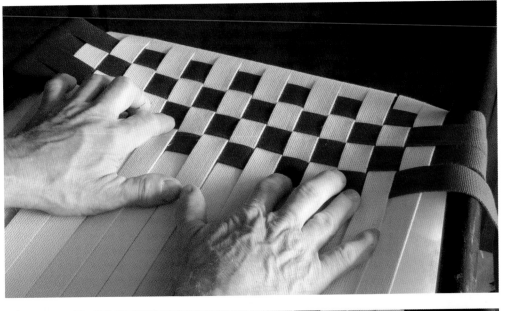

PHOTO 9 It's important to periodically push the weavers gently back to counter their natural inclination to creep toward the front rung in the middle of the seat.

PHOTO 10 About halfway to the front seat rung, it becomes difficult to force the coil of weaver between the shortened alternating strands of warp.

PHOTO 11 I switch to this big oak needle, passing the lead end of the weaver through the needle's eye and taping it in place.

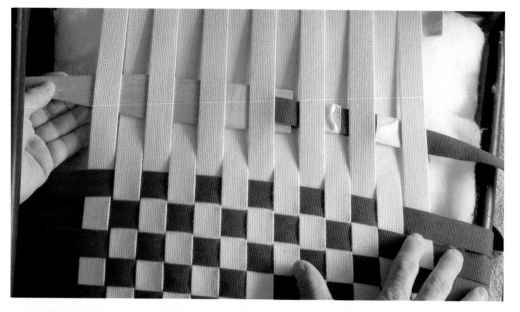

PHOTO 12 You can do the weaving without the needle, but I find it quicker and easier to use this weaving aide.

PHOTO 13 Traditionally, the ends of the gusset strips were sewn to the warp strands to keep them in place. The end of this gusset strip is held in place with a $1/4"$ staple driven into the side seat rung.

PHOTO 14 This detail shows how the staple was placed so that it is hidden when the weaver is in its proper position.

PHOTO 15 I think it's difficult to tell my stapled tape seat from the more traditionally installed sewn tape seat.

PHOTO 16 On the back side of the chair back, you can see the staples holding the two ends of the weaver in place.

PHOTO 17 Tape is also available in $^5/_8$" widths, a variety I used for the seat of this Pleasant Hill sewing rocker.

12

Weaving Rush Seats

Although I've woven hundreds of splint seats and probably hundreds of tape seats as well, I don't have much experience with rush. For several years, in fact, when a customer wanted a rush seat on a chair I'd made, they purchased the chair unseated from me and then took it to a seat weaver for the application of rush, but I like the look of a rush seat, so I have begun to weave my own.

Traditional rush is made from twisted cattail leaves. These leaves are cut in the fall, dried, then dampened prior to use. This is a very time-consuming process, one few customers want to pay for. While it's possible to purchase a product called *natural rush* which "resembles cattail rush," I've chosen to work with another alternative, a product called *fiber rush*, which is nothing more than a twisted strand of paper. The virtues of fiber rush are its ease of use, its consistent quality and it is readily available. It's stronger than you would expect a twist of paper to be. (It is not intended for outdoor use.)

The average chair seat takes about 2 pounds of fiber rush. For the two chairs in this book, I ordered a 10-pound reel of ⁵/₃₂" golden brown fiber rush from The Country Seat, Inc., www.thecountryseat.com (610-756-6124) which contained enough

PHOTO 1 Rush weaving requires only a handful of tools. I'll explain how these are used as we go.

PHOTO 2 I'm measuring to determine the central rectangle. The little flecks of white primer on the front rung are the results of the knife cuts I made to establish the front section of the seat's central rectangle. The distance between those flecks is the same as the length of the back rung between the back posts. Notice how rough the seat rungs are. When I turned them, I stopped after using the roughing gouge because the irregular surface keeps rush strands from slipping out of place on the seat rungs.

material to do the seats of both of the Arts & Crafts chairs in this book, with enough left over to do one more.

Before you start weaving, you must square up the seat to identify the limits of the gussets, those triangular sections of the seat on either side of the central rectangle. Measure the length of the back seat rung between the back posts. Then measure the length of the front seat rung between the front posts. Subtract the first length from the second. Divide the result by two and measure the resulting distance in from each end of the front posts on the front rung.

With the locations defined, it's time to cut the rush. Cut enough material for the first gusset strand. It should be approximately long enough to equal the length of the front rung and both side rungs. Each successive gusset strand needs to be a little longer than the one before.

Photos 4 and 5 show how to start the rush for the gussets. You must keep tension on each gusset strand (and later each weaving strand). A loose seat is unsightly, and tightness doesn't accumulate across a rush seat the way it does across a splint seat.

PHOTO 3 Here's a tip to make things easier: Mist the gusset strand with water to soften it before weaving.

PHOTO 4 Tack one end of the first gusset strand a couple of inches behind the left front post (left when you're facing the chair) onto the inside surface of the left side seat rung. Run that strand forward over the front seat rung, under the rung, over the gusset strand and the side seat rung and around the side seat rung. After coming up from the bottom of that rung, continue across the chair toward the opposite side seat rung.

PHOTO 5 The first gusset strand should continue over the right side seat rung. Wrap it around that rung, bring it up over itself and around the front seat rung just inside of the front post. Tack it to the inside of the side seat rung a couple of inches back from the front post.

PHOTO 6 Continue adding gusset strands in this way, starting each one 3/4"- 1" behind the start of the previous strand. After each strand, pull the weave toward the post as I'm doing here so the gusset strands will form 90° angles where they cross inside the seat rungs.

PHOTO 7 This is what the seat should look like when you're halfway through with the gusset strands. Notice that diagonals are beginning to form where the strands cross inside each corner.

PHOTO 8 The gusset strips have been completed. I have a slight gap to the outside of the white mark on the left end of the front seat rung, but it's not enough of a problem to try and squeeze in another gusset strand. It's time to begin the weaving strand.

PHOTO 9 First cut 15 - 25' of rush and moisten it. (I cut two such lengths so I can have one softening while I work the other. Each time I cut a new length, I moisten it and set it aside and work with the previously moistened length.) Tack one end of the weaving strand behind the start of the last gusset strand. (In the case of this chair, I tacked my weaving strand to the post because I'd run out of side seat rung.) Then wrap the weaving strand over the front seat rung and the left side seat rung in the same manner you previously wrapped each of the gusset strands. Continue across the front of the seat to the right side seat rung, wrapping it the same as you wrapped each of the gusset strands.

PHOTO 10 When you reach the back end of the right side seat rung, wrap it over the back seat rung, then around the back rung, up over itself and the side seat rung and run it back to the left back post.

PHOTO 11 Continue the wrap by passing the strand over the side seat rung, then up from underneath and over itself, around the back seat rung, then up from underneath and back to the front. This is the weaving pattern you will follow for most of the rest of the seat.

PHOTO 12 Keep as much tension as you can in every strand. Be sure to use a spring clamp to hold the tension if you leave the chair for any reason during the weaving process.

PHOTO 13 Use a knot to attach additional lengths of weavers. Make sure you tie these knots on the parts of the weaver that will be out of sight on the bottom of the seat.

PHOTO 14 Test the knot with a strong pull before you continue the weave.

PHOTO 15 Keep the new rows of weavers pulled back at each corner so that the advancing weavers form right angles where they cross.

PHOTO 16 As you approach the center of the seat, start to pack cardboard triangles into each of the four pockets formed by the weave. The object is to fill these pockets with enough cardboard so the weave around each pocket is taut. The cardboard fillers should be cut so that the grain of the cardboard is parallel with the seat rung against which the cardboard will be aligned. At this point, I pack in four layers of cardboard. Later, as I get close to the finish, I'll add one more layer of smaller cardboard triangles.

PHOTO 17   A good seat has a very tight weave, so it's imperative that you tighten the weaver at each wrap of each post. Notice the spring clamp on the right side seat rung. That clamp retains tension until I get the next length of weaver sufficiently tight.

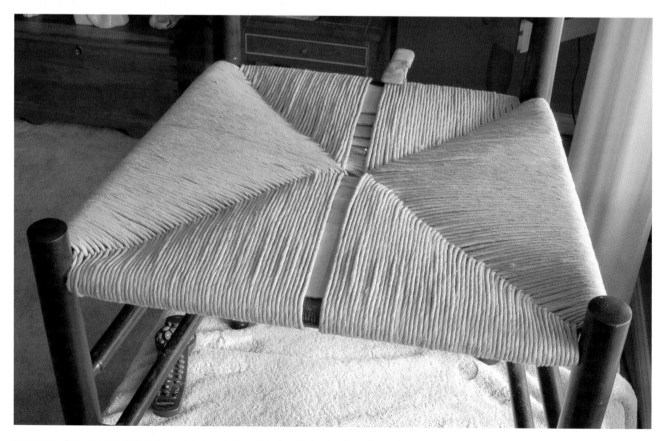

PHOTO 18   Because the seat is wider side-to-side than it is front-to-back, when I have the two side triangles filled, I still have an unfilled section in the width of the chair.

PHOTO 19 After filling in the last gap in the two side triangles, continue the weave until the weaver wraps over the top of the back rung. Then bring it forward up through the small hole in the middle of the seat. Continue on over the front seat rung, then come up through the hole in the middle of the seat, pass over the back seat rung and back up through the center hole beside the most recent pass.

What you're doing is creating a figure eight with your weaver with one loop of the eight encircling the back rung and the other loop of the eight encircling the front rung. The strand that creates these loops crosses in the hole in the middle of the seat.

PHOTO 20 In this close-up of the center of the seat, you can see where the figure-eight strands cross. There are five of these strands coming up from the bottom of the picture and four coming down from the top. Notice that I've alternated the directions of the strands to give the center of the seat an organized appearance.

PHOTO 21 Fiber rush is an easy-to-weave and inexpensive alternative to traditional rush. After the seat has been woven, lightly sand the painted surfaces of the chair and carefully apply a coat of paint to the chair's wood frame. This will remove any scuffings left by the seat weaving process.

Chairs with Rectangular Seats

Stools

Post-and-rung chairs can be divided into two basic types. One type includes those chairs with side rungs 90° from the front rungs (and back rungs as well). These constructions we refer to as stools. Because of this straight-forward construction method, they are simpler to build and simpler to seat than chairs with trapezoidal seats.

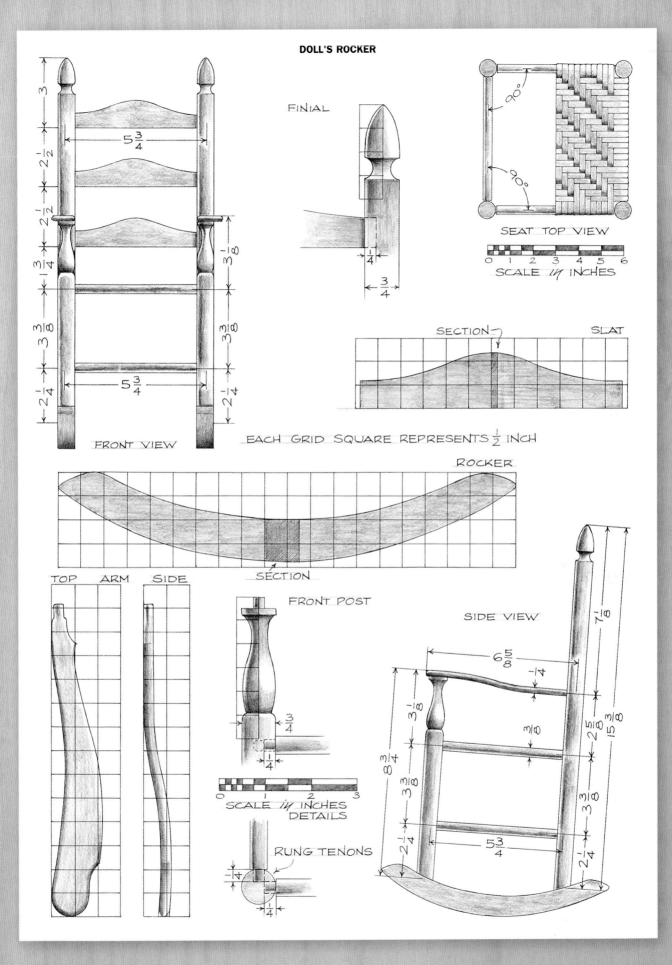

FINIAL

SEAT TOP VIEW

0 1 2 3 4 5 6
SCALE *in* INCHES

SECTION SLAT

EACH GRID SQUARE REPRESENTS $\frac{1}{2}$ INCH

FRONT VIEW

ROCKER

SECTION

TOP ARM SIDE

FRONT POST

SIDE VIEW

0 1 2 3
SCALE *in* INCHES
DETAILS

RUNG TENONS

105

New Lebanon Stool

Ejner Handberg, who immigrated to the United States from Denmark at the age of 17, worked for many year repairing and restoring Shaker furniture for several prominent early collectors, among them Mr. & Mrs. Edward Deming Edwards. Before returning repaired pieces to their owners, he did measured drawings of each one. These drawings have been collected and published by The Berkshire Traveller Press.

This stool is a reproduction of a New Lebanon Shaker stool drawn by Enjer Handberg. Its height makes it a little uncomfortable for use as a footstool, but it's just right for sitting.

This view of the New Lebanon stool from above shows the weaving pattern.

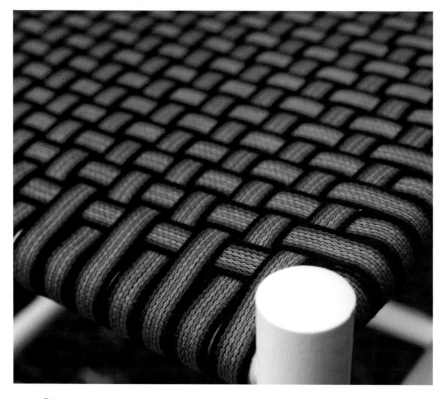

I used $5/8$" Shaker tape on this New Lebanon stool. Although this pattern is no longer available, there are still companies making similar $5/8$" tapes.

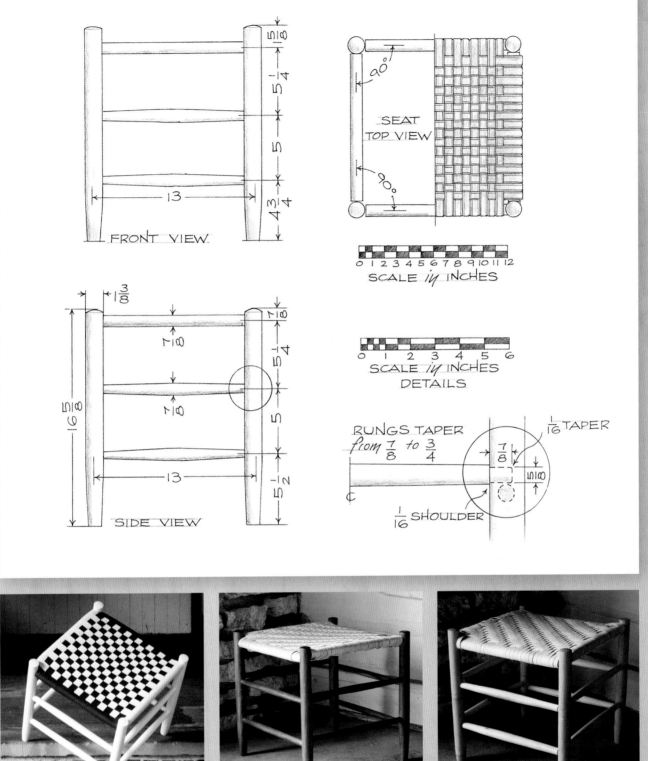

FRONT VIEW

SEAT TOP VIEW

SCALE in INCHES

SCALE in INCHES
DETAILS

SIDE VIEW

RUNGS TAPER from 7/8 to 3/4

1/16 TAPER

1/16 SHOULDER

Above are three variations of the stool shown at the top of the page. The posts of all are identical, though there are differences in the rung lengths. At the left, the checkerboard pattern is achieved by using two different colors of tape for the weave, one color running from front to back, the other color running from side to side. In the middle is the same stool made of walnut (the painted stool is made of maple). At right is a third example of this form, this time in natural maple. Notice how different each of these three versions looks, despite the fact that each is essentially the same form.

107

Splint-Back Bar Stool

I know. There's something wrong about making a *bar* stool using Shaker design elements, but I wanted one piece that had the primary components of a chair — seat and back — that could be made quickly and easily by a relatively inexperienced chairmaker, so I added this bar stool to the collection appearing in the book.

(I might also mention that the Shakers made, consumed and sold alcoholic beverages.)

The rectangular shapes of the seat and back, as well as the absence of any steam-bent parts, make this an excellent jumping off point for someone looking to try a post-and-rung chair.

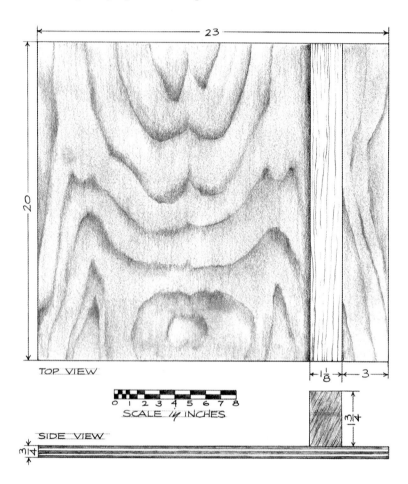

TOP VIEW

23

20

1⅛

3

SCALE ⅓ INCHES
0 1 2 3 4 5 6 7 8

SIDE VIEW

¾

¾

When you're preparing to drill the side-rung mortises, set the fence of the jig so that it's a distance from the lead point of your Forstner bit that's half the diameter of the post. In this case, the fence is being set for a post a bit less than 1¹/2" in diameter.

The stool's front ladder rests on the jig while I bring the bit down into the post. I'm using the jig shown above to aligh the ladder under the drill bit.

108

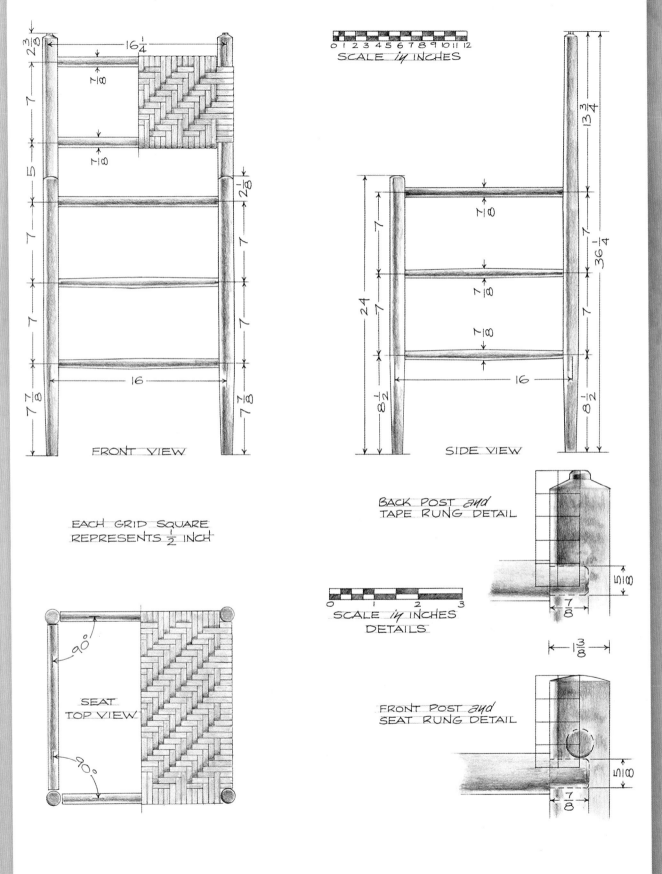

FRONT VIEW

SIDE VIEW

SCALE in INCHES

EACH GRID SQUARE
REPRESENTS ½ INCH

BACK POST and
TAPE RUNG DETAIL

SCALE in INCHES
DETAILS

SEAT
TOP VIEW

FRONT POST and
SEAT RUNG DETAIL

Arts & Crafts and Union Village Stools

These two stools are very close in their construction details, so I'm presenting them together.

The Arts & Crafts stool (at right) is one I designed specifically for use with the Gimson-style Arts & Crafts chair. Like the Gimson chair, this stool is seated with rush.

The Warren County Museum in Lebanon, Ohio, maintains an important collection of Shaker furniture produced in communities once located in Southwest Ohio. This Union Village stool (below) is one piece in the museum's collection.

PHOTO BY AL PARRISH, THANKS TO THE WARREN COUNTY HISTORICAL MUSEUM

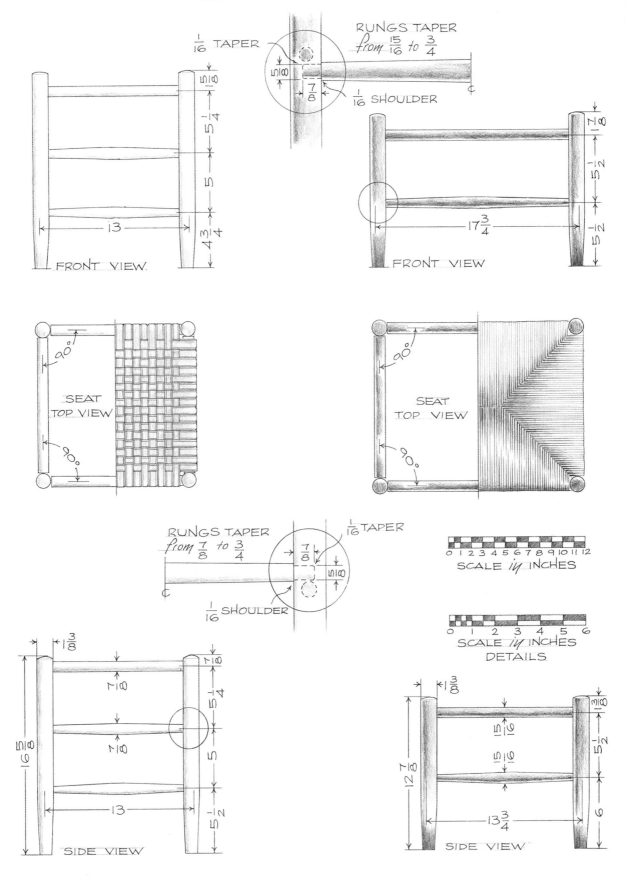

$\frac{1}{16}$ TAPER

RUNGS TAPER *from* $\frac{15}{16}$ to $\frac{3}{4}$

$\frac{5}{8}$

$\frac{7}{8}$

$\frac{1}{16}$ SHOULDER

C

FRONT VIEW

$15\frac{1}{8}$

$5\frac{1}{4}$

5

13

$4\frac{3}{4}$

$1\frac{7}{8}$

$5\frac{1}{2}$

$17\frac{3}{4}$

$5\frac{1}{2}$

FRONT VIEW

90°

SEAT
TOP VIEW

90°

90°

SEAT
TOP VIEW

90°

RUNGS TAPER *from* $\frac{7}{8}$ to $\frac{3}{4}$

$\frac{1}{16}$ TAPER

$\frac{7}{8}$

$\frac{5}{8}$

C

$\frac{1}{16}$ SHOULDER

0 1 2 3 4 5 6 7 8 9 10 11 12
SCALE *in* INCHES

0 1 2 3 4 5 6
SCALE *in* INCHES
DETAILS

$\frac{3}{8}$

$\frac{7}{8}$

$\frac{7}{8}$

$16\frac{5}{8}$

13

$1\frac{7}{8}$

$5\frac{1}{4}$

5

$5\frac{1}{2}$

SIDE VIEW

$\frac{3}{8}$

$\frac{15}{16}$

$\frac{15}{16}$

$12\frac{7}{8}$

$13\frac{3}{4}$

$1\frac{3}{8}$

$5\frac{1}{2}$

6

SIDE VIEW

111

14

Chairs with Trapezoidal Seats

Most chairs in the Shaker universe (and elsewhere) have trapezoidal seats. The front and back rungs are parallel while the side rungs taper toward the back. The triangles these tapering side rungs form on each side of a chair's central rectangle are called gussets.

This chapter features a number of chairs with trapezoidal seats. Some chairs are presented with construction information specific to those forms, while other chairs are represented with only photos and drawings because the construction of those chairs is comprehensively represented by the information in Chapters 1-12.

Shown at extreme left is, in my judgment, the most comfortable side chair ever made by the Shakers or anyone else, for that matter. Slat-backs are uncomfortable for long periods of sitting. In fact, they are so uncomfortable that the New Lebanon Shakers sometimes sold cushions that could be tied to a slat-back chair's cushion rail to ameliorate this discomfort. The New Lebanon #5 tape-back chair shown here addresses this issue more directly by eliminating the slats (except for a single decorative slat above the chair back/human back contact area) and replacing it with a cushioned tape panel.

The acorn finial in the left photo is from a New Lebanon No. 6 slat-back. It is different than the acorn finial from a New Lebanon No. 5 tape back in the right photo. This basic shape appeared in many variations during the era of New Lebanon chairmaking.

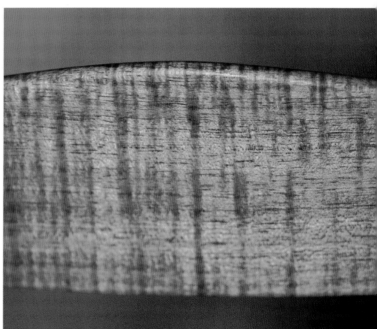

This slat's simple shape provides an effective setting for the Australian curly blackwood.

To highlight the figured maple, I applied a wash of aniline dye before finishing this chair.

New Lebanon #5 Tape-back Chair

While it's very easy to bend $1/4$" thick slats to accomdate a human back, it's more difficult to bend a 1"-thick rung. However, with a couple of technical accommodations, it is possible to achieve successful results with these thicker components. First, as you can see in Photo 5, I don't impose as acute a bend on rungs. Second, I reduce the thickness of these components.

PHOTO 1 After turning the tape bars to a 1" diameter, I plane much of the thickness from two opposing sides of each bar until I have a bar that's a bit less than $5/8$" thick. I then bend that bar, and I rarely have any failures. I'm holding the bar in a vise to plane one side. Then I'll then rotate the bar 180° and plane a flat on the other side.

PHOTO 2 These two bars have been prepared for bending. The flats need to be planed on precisely opposite sides of each bar. (The tenons are $1/2$" in diameter, unlike the $5/8$" tenons on the other rungs.)

PHOTO 4 I use an awl to make a starter hole for the lead tip of my Forstner bit. This starter hole should be about $3/16$" behind the back post's center line. This placement of the mortises for the tape-bar tenons is discussed in the mortising chapter.

PHOTO 3 Experience tells me that this is about as far as I can push a steamed tape bar without any risk of breaking. I also know that this is enough of a bend to make the back of this chair comfortable.

PHOTO 5 It would be best to have a pair of spotters when you're free-handing a mortise angle: one to stand behind you and align the 90° angle and one on the left to sight the top of the chair's ladder, but I always work alone and the process is very forgiving.

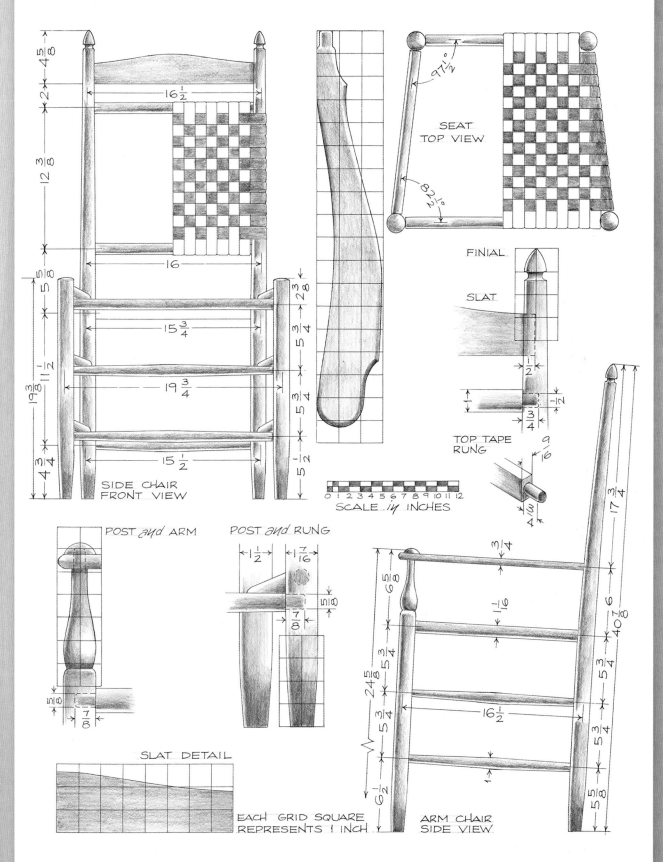

SEAT
TOP VIEW

FINIAL

SLAT

TOP TAPE
RUNG

SIDE CHAIR
FRONT VIEW

SCALE IN INCHES

POST and ARM

POST and RUNG

SLAT DETAIL

EACH GRID SQUARE
REPRESENTS 1 INCH

ARM CHAIR
SIDE VIEW

New Lebanon #6 Slat-back Arm Chair and #6 Slat-back Side Chair

I've made dozens — perhaps hundreds — of #6 dining chairs, and many of my customers choose the arm appearing below — an arm I designed — rather than the arm that appeared on the Shaker originals. The original #6 arm is a slightly longer version of the arm appearing on page 115.

For someone my size (6', 190 pounds) the #6 is a good choice, but for someone a few inches shorter, the #5 shown on the preceding pages is preferable.

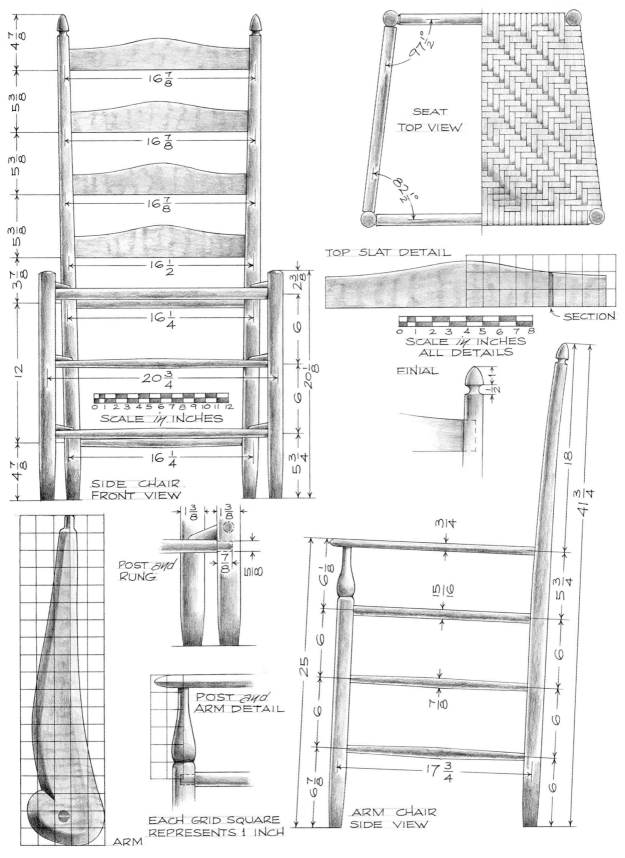

$4\frac{7}{8}$

$5\frac{3}{8}$

$5\frac{3}{8}$

$5\frac{3}{8}$

$3\frac{7}{8}$

12

$4\frac{7}{8}$

$16\frac{7}{8}$

$16\frac{7}{8}$

$16\frac{7}{8}$

$16\frac{1}{2}$

$16\frac{1}{4}$

$20\frac{3}{4}$

$16\frac{1}{4}$

SCALE *in* INCHES
0 1 2 3 4 5 6 7 8 9 10 11 12

SIDE CHAIR
FRONT VIEW

$2\frac{3}{8}$

6

6

6

$5\frac{3}{4}$

$20\frac{1}{8}$

$97\frac{1}{2}°$

$71\frac{1}{2}°$

SEAT
TOP VIEW

TOP SLAT DETAIL

SECTION

SCALE *in* INCHES
0 1 2 3 4 5 6 7 8
ALL DETAILS

FINIAL

$\frac{1}{2}$

18

$41\frac{3}{4}$

$5\frac{3}{4}$

POST *and*
RUNG

$1\frac{3}{8}$ $1\frac{3}{8}$

$\frac{7}{8}$

$5\frac{1}{8}$

POST *and*
ARM DETAIL

ARM

EACH GRID SQUARE
REPRESENTS 1 INCH

$3\frac{1}{4}$

$6\frac{1}{8}$

$15\frac{1}{16}$

$7\frac{1}{8}$

25

6

6

6

$6\frac{7}{8}$

6

6

6

6

$17\frac{3}{4}$

ARM CHAIR
SIDE VIEW

New Lebanon Transitional Rocker

This is based on a transitional rocker made at the New Lebanon chair shop in the middle of the 19th century. It's referred to as transitional because it was built during the period when the New Lebanon chair operation was shifting from individually made chairs fabricated in a woodshop to mass-produced chairs fabricated in a factory.

My current version of this chair (at right) differs from the original in several details. First, I have a vase rather than a simple taper under the arm. Second, I moved the back posts closer together at the cushion rail, in order to increase the verticality of the back ladder. And finally, I increased the width of the arm and added a crowned bevel to the arm's perimeter.

Both of these chairs are New Lebanon transitional rockers. The only difference is the material. Black walnut on the left and hard maple on the right.

This detail of the chair shows the bend in the slats as well as the cushion rail at the top of the chair's ladder. The cushion rail was added as a mooring point for the heavy cushions Shakers often sold with ladder backs.

The back posts terminate in wedged tenons that pass through the cushion rail. In this photo, you can just see the wedged, through tenon.

This close-up of the arm shows the crowned bevel. This crowned feature accomplishes two things. First, it's more comfortable than the narrower, cookie-cutter shape of the original arm, and second, it has a more contemporary look, placing this chair in the 20th or 21st rather than in the 19th century.

118

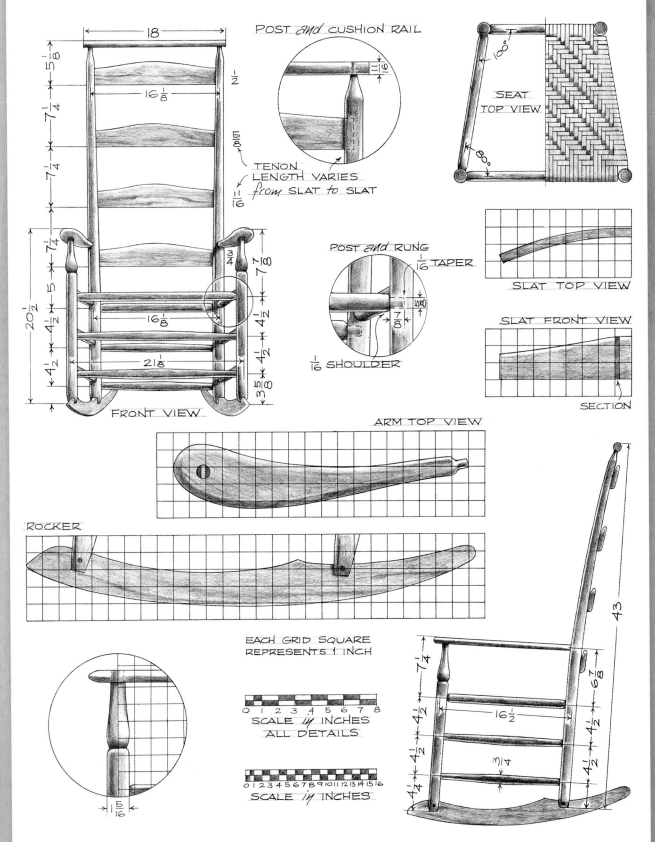

POST *and* CUSHION RAIL

TENON LENGTH VARIES *from* SLAT TO SLAT

SEAT TOP VIEW

100°

80°

POST *and* RUNG

$\frac{1}{16}$ TAPER

$\frac{1}{16}$ SHOULDER

SLAT TOP VIEW

SLAT FRONT VIEW

SECTION

FRONT VIEW

18

$16\frac{1}{8}$

$16\frac{1}{8}$

$21\frac{1}{8}$

$5\frac{5}{8}$

$7\frac{1}{4}$

$7\frac{1}{4}$

$7\frac{1}{4}$

5

$4\frac{1}{2}$

$4\frac{1}{2}$

$20\frac{1}{2}$

$\frac{3}{4}$

$7\frac{7}{8}$

$4\frac{1}{2}$

$4\frac{1}{2}$

$3\frac{5}{8}$

$2\frac{1}{2}$

$3\frac{1}{8}$

$1\frac{1}{16}$

$1\frac{1}{16}$

$\frac{11}{16}$

$7\frac{8}{}$

$\frac{5}{8}$

ARM TOP VIEW

ROCKER

EACH GRID SQUARE
REPRESENTS 1 INCH

0 1 2 3 4 5 6 7 8

SCALE *in* INCHES
ALL DETAILS

0 1 2 3 4 5 6 7 8 9 10 11 12 13 14 15 16

SCALE *in* INCHES

$\frac{5}{16}$

43

$7\frac{1}{4}$

$6\frac{7}{8}$

$16\frac{1}{2}$

$4\frac{1}{2}$

$4\frac{1}{2}$

$4\frac{1}{2}$

$4\frac{1}{2}$

$4\frac{1}{4}$

$3\frac{1}{4}$

119

New Lebanon #1 Rocker with Tape-and-Slat Back

The chairs produced in the New Lebanon Shaker chairmaking operation were graduated in seven sizes. #7 being the largest for large adults and #1 being the smallest for young children.

PHOTOS BY AL PARRISH, THANKS TO THE
WARREN COUNTY HISTORICAL MUSEUM

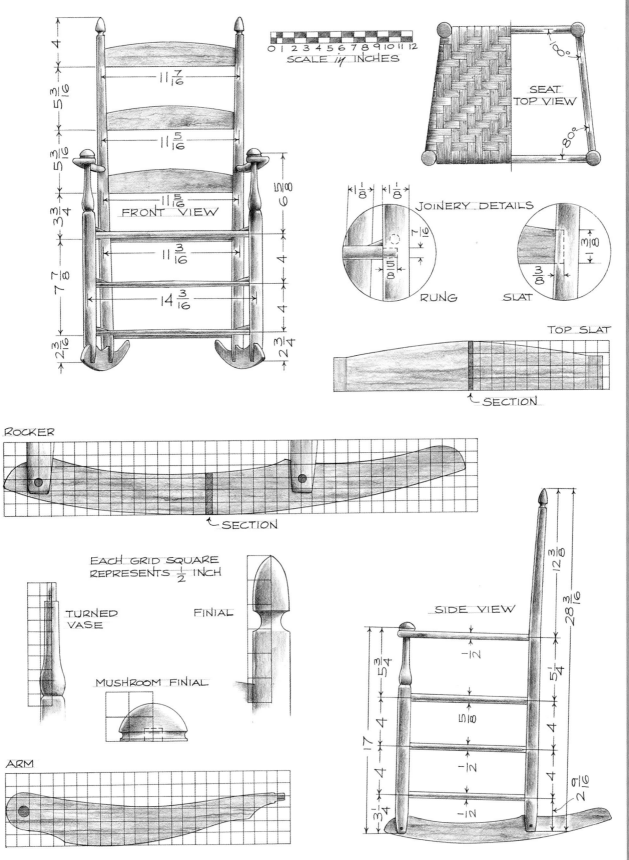

SCALE in INCHES

FRONT VIEW

SEAT TOP VIEW

JOINERY DETAILS

RUNG   SLAT

TOP SLAT

SECTION

ROCKER

SECTION

EACH GRID SQUARE
REPRESENTS ½ INCH

TURNED VASE

FINIAL

MUSHROOM FINIAL

SIDE VIEW

ARM

Union Village Four-slat Side Chair

Because contemporary Americans are larger than their 19th-century ancestors, most of the chairs designed and used by those ancestors look doll-like in size. I can sit in this chair (I'm 6' tall and weigh 190 pounds) but I look a little goofy doing it. Therefore, when I make Shaker reproductions for my customers built more like me than our 19th century ancestors, I typically scale them up in size.

This chair has one feature that makes it different from all but two other chairs in this book — the flats located on the front side of the back posts. It also has a feature not shared by any other chair in this book. The chair is a *tilter*.

In the Shaker universe, the tilter concept was manifested in two ways. Some tilters included a patented foot that was attached to a rotating ball mounted inside the bottom of each back post. This ball rotated as the sitter leaned back in the chair so that the foot remained

The clipped-corner slat is one of the signatures of Union Village chairs.

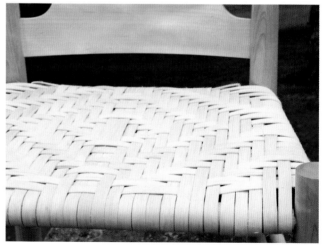

Because splint is stiff enough to retain its shape over time, I don't stuff the seats of splint-bottomed chairs.

122

in solid contact with the floor no matter how far back the sitter leaned in the chair. The other, perhaps more important manifestation of the tilter (the one present in this chair) is that the center lines of the side rungs and the center lines of the posts are not at 90° angles, as is the case with every other chair in this book.

To be comfortable, a chair needs to have a slight backward tilt. This can be achieved in two different ways. The most common method is to place the side rungs so that their points of entry into the back posts are lower than their corresponding points of entry into the front posts. This imposes a backward tilt on the chair.

The other method (the one used by a fair number of Shaker and non-Shaker chairs) is to modify the angles at which the side rungs enter the front and back posts. If you look at this chair from the side, you will see that the angle formed by the side seat rung and the back post is less than 90° (when measured below the seat) and the angle formed by that same seat rung and the front post is more than 90°.

PHOTO 1 The back posts are first turned round, just like every other back post of every other chair in this book.

PHOTO 2 After the posts have been marked, lock the lathe's rotation, and rough in the flat on the front of the back post with a drawknife, paying close attention to grain direction. (You must first mark the post for the drilling of rung mortises because that's how you'll establish which side of the post is the front.) Notice that the flat is not fully facing the front. Instead, it's turned slightly inward. You may be able to see also that I've lightly sketched the limits of the flat in pencil.

PHOTO 3 I then remounted the post in a bench vise for finish shaping with a spokeshave, scraper and sandpaper, although I could have done this with the post still in the lathe.

PHOTO 4 Drill front and back rung mortises exactly as you did for the other post-and-rung chairs in this book. (I used tape to secure the post to the FRMJ because the taper at the bottom of the post would have caused my locking screws to chip the bottom of the posts.)

PHOTO 5 This is the setting I used on the drill-press table to achieve this chair's backward tilt, just 3° off the perpendicular. Most tilters have a more pronounced backward lean than does this example. Before you attempt this, take some time to get the angles clear in your head and remember that the side rung mortises on one side of the back ladder will be drilled with the table slanting in one direction, while the side-rung mortises on the other side of that same ladder will be drilled with the table slanted in the other direction. The same rule applies to drilling the front ladder.

PHOTO 6 Notice that I've set the SRMJ so that the posts aren't crowded against the fence. It's a bit easier to set up this way, but it does require you to control the alignment of the ladder freehand.

PHOTO 7 Don't forget to check the depth of each mortise.

124

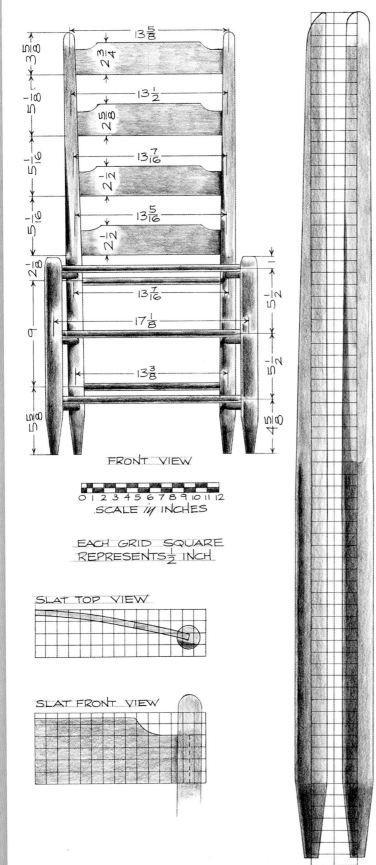

FRONT VIEW

SCALE IN INCHES

EACH GRID SQUARE
REPRESENTS ½ INCH

SLAT TOP VIEW

SLAT FRONT VIEW

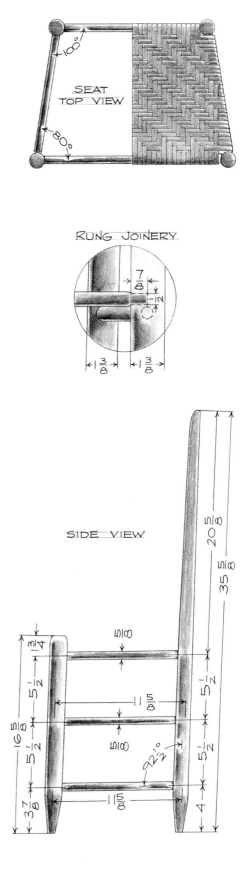

SEAT
TOP VIEW

RUNG JOINERY

SIDE VIEW

Union Village Two-slat Dining Chair

The Shakers in Ohio and elsewhere made a number of variations of this two-slat chair. The short back ladder permitted the chair to be pushed completely under the dining table in order to make floor sweeping easier.

The color is my addition, although the Shakers frequently painted the interiors of their living quarters and their furniture — including some chairs — in bold colors.

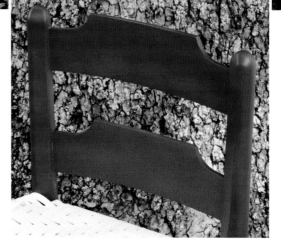

This example features the clipped corners on the slats typical of Union Village chairs.

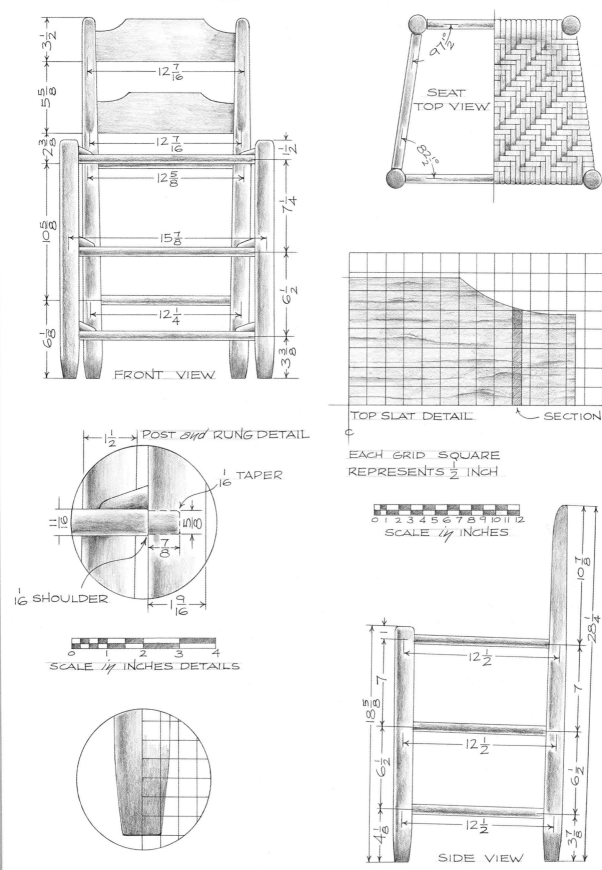

FRONT VIEW

$3\frac{1}{2}$

$5\frac{5}{8}$

$2\frac{3}{8}$

$10\frac{5}{8}$

$6\frac{1}{8}$

$12\frac{7}{16}$

$12\frac{7}{16}$

$12\frac{5}{8}$

$15\frac{7}{8}$

$12\frac{1}{4}$

$1\frac{1}{2}$

$7\frac{1}{4}$

$6\frac{1}{2}$

$3\frac{3}{8}$

SEAT TOP VIEW

$97\frac{1}{2}°$

$82\frac{1}{2}°$

TOP SLAT DETAIL   SECTION

EACH GRID SQUARE
REPRESENTS $\frac{1}{2}$ INCH

POST *and* RUNG DETAIL

$1\frac{1}{2}$

$\frac{1}{16}$ TAPER

$\frac{11}{16}$

$\frac{5}{8}$

$\frac{7}{8}$

$1\frac{9}{16}$

$\frac{1}{16}$ SHOULDER

0 1 2 3 4 5 6 7 8 9 10 11 12
SCALE *in* INCHES

0   1   2   3   4
SCALE *in* INCHES DETAILS

SIDE VIEW

$10\frac{7}{8}$

$28\frac{1}{4}$

$18\frac{5}{8}$

$6\frac{1}{2}$

$4\frac{1}{8}$

1

7

$12\frac{1}{2}$

$12\frac{1}{2}$

$12\frac{1}{2}$

7

$6\frac{1}{2}$

$3\frac{7}{8}$

127

Union Village Four-slat Rocker

The Union Village Shaker original on which this reproduction is based had a heavier look than does my version. The arms lack the crowned bevels you see here. They are instead simply bandsawn shapes with the edges left square to the top and bottom surfaces. Also, the front posts on the original are heavier than the front posts you see here. While I like the lines of the original chair and the very deep seat, I was less taken with the overall heaviness of that original. Please note, the drawing on page 129 represents the original chair, not my variation.

I added crowned bevels to the perimeter of the arms on the chair and a wedged through-tenon at the top of each front post.

On the original four-slat Union Village rocker, I felt the balls atop the finials were strangely undersized for the tops of the heavy back posts, so I doubled the size of those balls.

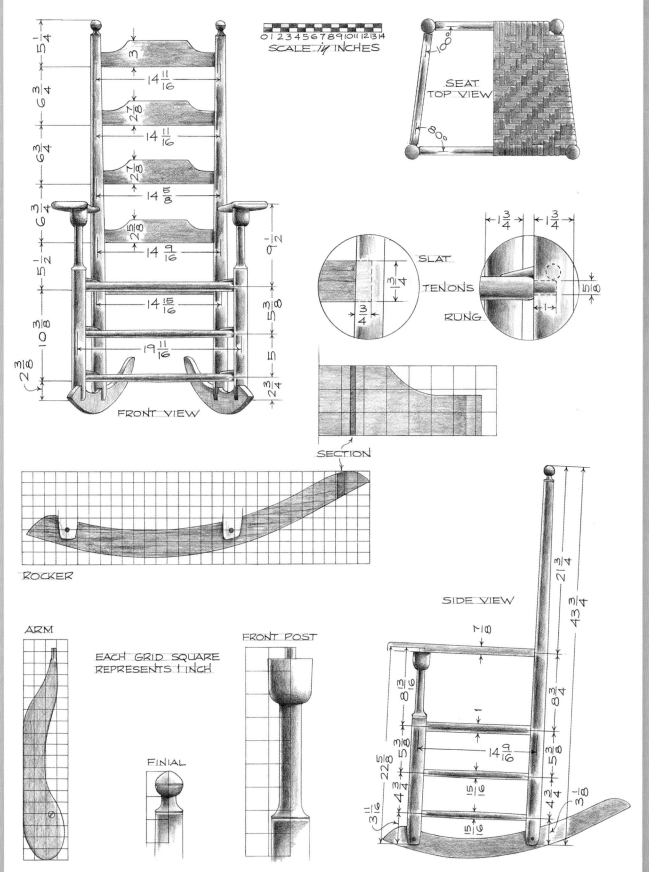

SCALE *in* INCHES

SEAT
TOP VIEW

FRONT VIEW

SLAT

TENONS

RUNG

SECTION

ROCKER

SIDE VIEW

ARM

EACH GRID SQUARE
REPRESENTS 1 INCH

FINIAL

FRONT POST

Splint-back Rocker

These two chairs — one done in walnut, the other in maple, with curly arms — are my designs, but I think it's easy to see in them the influence of 30 years of building Shaker chair reproductions.

These chairs are comfortable, despite the lack of bent back posts because the woven back panels yield when you lean up against them.

You can see the unbent back posts in this shot.

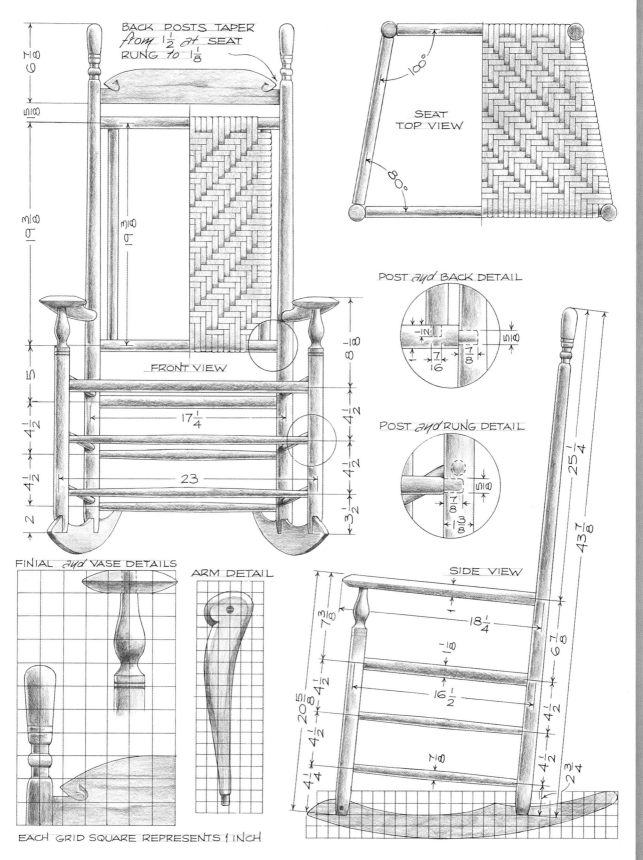

BACK POSTS TAPER *from* $1\frac{1}{2}$ *at* SEAT
RUNG *to* $1\frac{1}{8}$

$6\frac{7}{8}$

$1\frac{5}{8}$

$19\frac{3}{8}$

$19\frac{3}{8}$

SEAT TOP VIEW

100°

80°

FRONT VIEW

$8\frac{1}{8}$

5

$4\frac{1}{2}$

$4\frac{1}{2}$

2

$17\frac{1}{4}$

23

$4\frac{1}{2}$

$4\frac{1}{2}$

$3\frac{1}{2}$

POST *and* BACK DETAIL

$1\frac{1}{2}$

$\frac{7}{16}$

$\frac{7}{8}$

$5\frac{1}{8}$

POST *and* RUNG DETAIL

$\frac{7}{8}$

$\frac{3}{8}$

$5\frac{1}{8}$

$25\frac{1}{4}$

$43\frac{7}{8}$

SIDE VIEW

1

$18\frac{1}{4}$

$\frac{1}{8}$

$16\frac{1}{2}$

$6\frac{7}{8}$

$4\frac{1}{2}$

$4\frac{1}{2}$

$2\frac{3}{4}$

$7\frac{3}{8}$

$20\frac{5}{8}$

$4\frac{1}{2}$

$4\frac{1}{2}$

$4\frac{1}{4}$

$\frac{7}{8}$

FINIAL *and* VASE DETAILS

ARM DETAIL

EACH GRID SQUARE REPRESENTS 1 INCH

Designing a Chair

While I do produce some literal reproductions of Shaker originals, most of the chairs I build are modifications of those originals. As you can see from the other photo captions in this section, I will change a part if I think I can improve the chair by doing so. I'll widen an arm or give it a more sculpted look. I'll change a finial or the shape of the vase under the arm in order to make these details, at least in my judgment, more interesting or more balanced.

But sometimes, after many years of fiddling with a chair's details, I end up with a form that is so different from the original that the original is no longer visible in the chair. That's the case with this example.

Believe it or not, this chair has its genesis in the transitional rocker discussed earlier in this section (which is itself a variation of a Shaker original). The rockers are essentially the same as the rockers on that transitional rocker. So too are the side rungs. The front and back rungs, however, have been lengthened to make space for the woven back panel. The vases under the arms and the finials atop the back posts are not quite like anything in the Shaker universe, although both details are clearly rooted in the Shaker aesthetic. The arms, of course, are different than any Shaker arm.

This process of making incremental changes to a chair's design is the design process I follow when creating a new form. I don't sit down with paper and say that I'm going to design a chair of my own. I change a bit here and there on a Shaker original. Then, in my next edition of that chair, I make another change or two. And

more in the next and so on. What results over a period of years is a chair that isn't quite like anything that preceded it and is much different from the orginal form with which I began. The roots of the design are obscured by the proliferation of altered details.

I believe this is the design process practiced by the great 19th-century Shaker chairmakers. If you look at the history of chairs made in the New Lebanon chairmaking operation (for which there is a detailed photographic record), you can see the same incremental, accumulative process at work.

It's not like Brother Wagan, the reknowned New Lebanon chairmaker, sat down one day in 1855 and decided to design the great Shaker chair. The record suggests that he did just what I do, that is, he changed a couple of details here and there. And then on the next chair he changed a couple more.

Maple—the wood in this example—is a good choice for a chair that's likely to receive rough treatment because it is extremely strong.

The back slat of the chairs is decorated with an incised squiggle, and the finial with a pair of incised lines.

I carved the little squiggle with a chip-carving knife and a paring chisel.

I repeat the pair of incised lines from the finial just below the vases under the arms.

The arms of the chairs feature the crowned bevels around their perimeters that have become typical of my work.

Gimson-style Arts & Crafts Arm Chair

Ernest Gimson (1863-1919) was an English craftsman working in the Arts & Crafts tradition under
the influence of William Morris. When I was looking for pieces to include in this book, I happened
on a small black-and-white photo of a Gimson
arm chair that was not quite like anything I had
seen before. Unfortunately, I could find neither
a measured drawing of the chair nor a detailed
photograph (although even if I had, I probably
would have tinkered with the Gimson form), so I
scaled up a chair based on that small image. This
photo unites the Gimson-style chair and the stool
I designed to go with it.

Because I was working from such a small photo, I couldn't identify the specific details on the
Gimson original, but I could see a bit of turned detail on the front post under the arm and
another bit of turned detail above the seat. I could also see some sculpture on the arm,
although I couldn't pick out the details of that sculpture.

The arm on my Gimson-style chair conveys
a serpentine movement from the back to
the front.

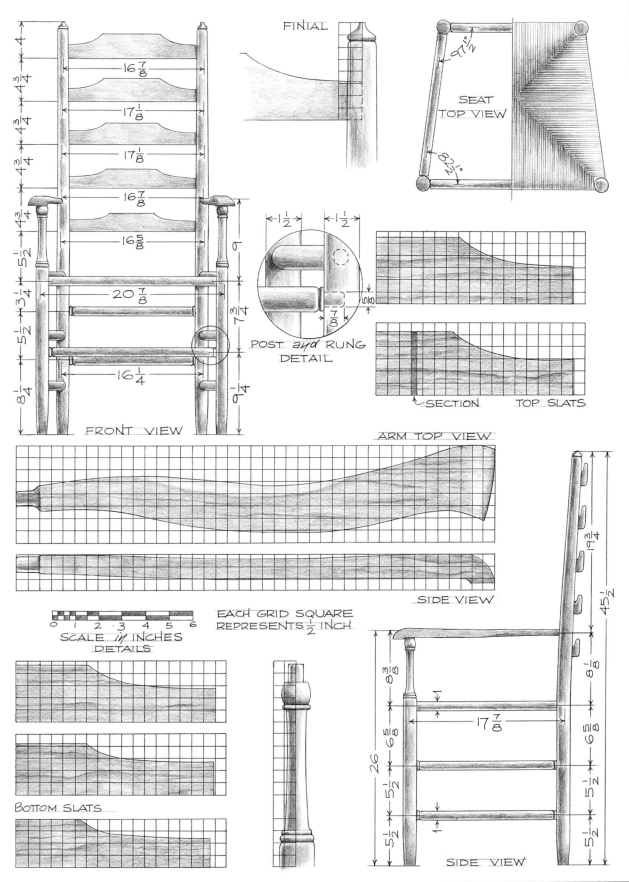

FINIAL

SEAT
TOP VIEW

97½°

82½°

POST *and* RUNG
DETAIL

SECTION   TOP SLATS

ARM TOP VIEW

FRONT VIEW

16⅞

17⅛

17⅛

16⅞

16⅝

20⅞

16¼

4

4¾

4¾

4¾

4¾

5½

3¼

5½

8¼

9

7¾

9¼

SIDE VIEW

SCALE *in* INCHES
DETAILS

EACH GRID SQUARE
REPRESENTS ½ INCH

BOTTOM SLATS

19¾

45½

8⅜

8⅛

17⅞

26

6⅝

6⅝

5½

5½

5½

5½

SIDE VIEW

135

I couldn't see whether the turned detail at the top and bottom of the Gimson vase was composed of coves or beads or a combination of the two. I chose to use beads as one of the unifying design elements in my version of this chair. These little beads are very delicate and can be destroyed by a single moment of inattention at the lathe, so be very careful with the tip of your skew. In fact, if you're not comfortable forming small beads on the lathe, it might be best to work on some of the other chairs in this book before attempting this Gimson-style chair.

Because other Arts & Crafts chairs I have seen have more acute bends on the back posts than do my Shaker reproductions, I made a new bending form for the back posts of the Gimson-style chair. The hose clamp I use to bend back posts isn't long enough to enclose the unbent posts on this new form, so I first used a pipe clamp to draw them partially together before putting the hose clamp in place. Also, I added the ⁵⁄₈"-diameter plugs in the seat-rung mortises because I was afraid the more acute bend might cause a blowout of some kind at their location.

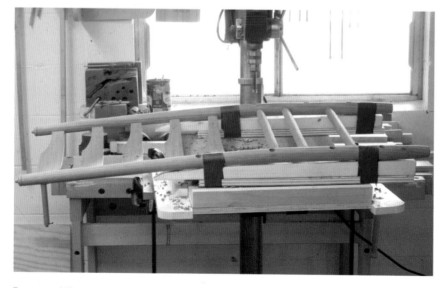

Because of the more acute bends of these back posts, I had to use bandsawn cauls taped to the back of the back posts in order to get the back ladder to sit properly on the SRMJ. The cauls don't need to be fit perfectly. They just need to allow the ladder to be securely positioned in approximately the correct position.

Unless you're experienced and confident on the bandsaw, I don't recommend that you use this technique for cutting the arms. It's dangerous to both the parts and your hands. You could safely form the arms with them clamped to your bench top so they could be worked with carving tools.

This is what the rough-shaped arm should look like.

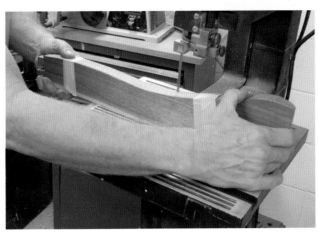

After you've cut the contour of the arm in the horizontal plane, tape the scraps to the blank and saw the sway on the top of the arm.

Finish shaping the arm with a drawknife, spokeshave and rasps while holding the arm in the pipe-clamp puppets I demonstrated in the arm-shaping chapter.

Clisset-style Arts & Crafts Side Chair

Phillip Clisset, born in 1817, became involved in the
English Arts & Crafts movement late in his life. The ladderbacks he created during that time now bear his name. This
is my version of a Clisset ladderback.

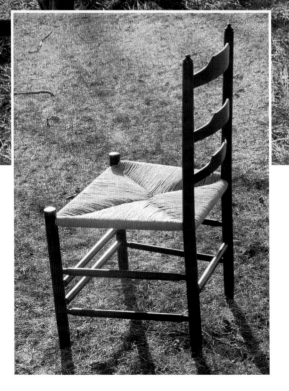

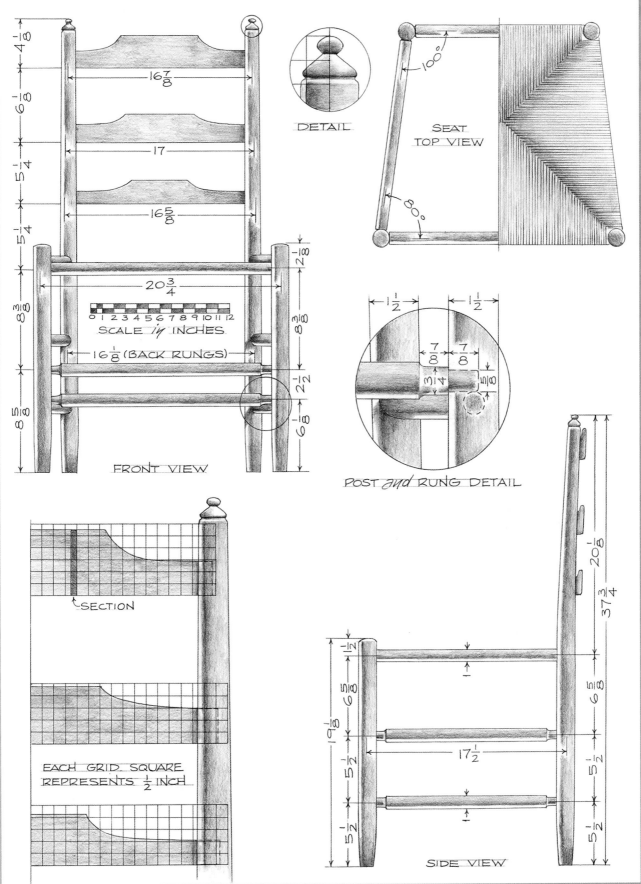

DETAIL

SEAT
TOP VIEW

$4\frac{1}{8}$

$6\frac{1}{8}$

$16\frac{7}{8}$

$5\frac{1}{4}$

17

$5\frac{1}{4}$

$16\frac{5}{8}$

$2\frac{1}{8}$

$20\frac{3}{4}$

$8\frac{3}{8}$

$8\frac{3}{8}$

SCALE *in* INCHES

$16\frac{1}{8}$ (BACK RUNGS)

$8\frac{5}{8}$

$2\frac{1}{2}$

$6\frac{1}{8}$

FRONT VIEW

$100°$

$80°$

$1\frac{1}{2}$

$1\frac{1}{2}$

$\frac{7}{8}$

$\frac{7}{8}$

$\frac{3}{4}$

$\frac{5}{8}$

POST *and* RUNG DETAIL

SECTION

EACH GRID SQUARE
REPRESENTS $\frac{1}{2}$ INCH

$20\frac{1}{8}$

$37\frac{3}{4}$

$1\frac{1}{2}$

$6\frac{5}{8}$

1

$6\frac{5}{8}$

$19\frac{1}{8}$

$5\frac{1}{2}$

$17\frac{1}{2}$

$5\frac{1}{2}$

$5\frac{1}{2}$

1

$5\frac{1}{2}$

SIDE VIEW

139

Country Side Chair

I wanted to include one country chair built by an anonymous maker who wasn't affiliated with the Shakers or the Arts & Crafts movement in order to demonstrate the close, almost familial kinship of these traditions. This simple ladderback is typical of tens of thousands of ladderbacks made by American country craftsmen. Notice how much it resembles the Shaker and Arts & Crafts examples in its engineering and design.

The original is seated with binder cane, which I don't discuss in this book, so the drawn representation features a Shaker-tape seat.

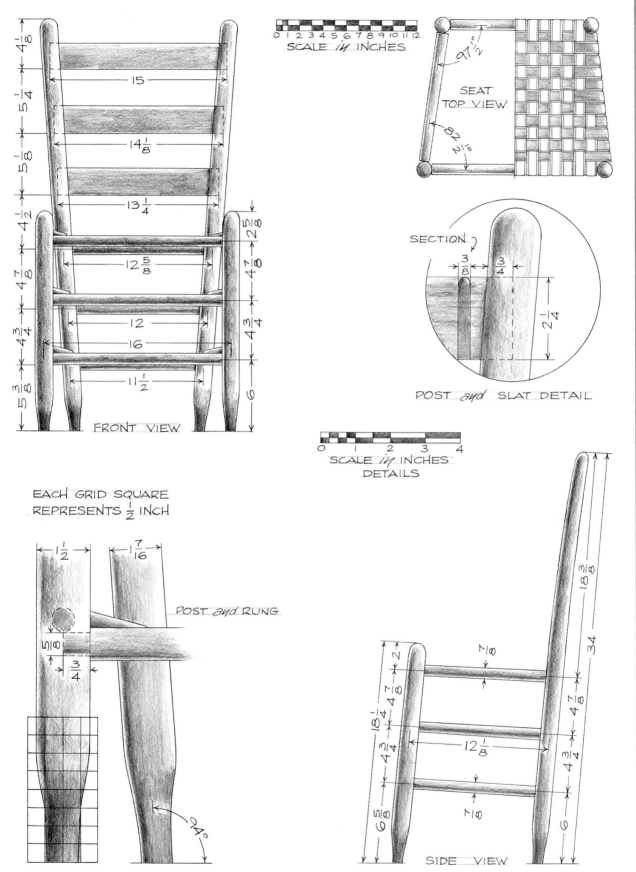

SCALE *in* INCHES

SEAT
TOP VIEW

SECTION

POST *and* SLAT DETAIL

SCALE *in* INCHES
DETAILS

FRONT VIEW

EACH GRID SQUARE
REPRESENTS $\frac{1}{2}$ INCH

POST *and* RUNG

SIDE VIEW

141

15

Hancock Bench

Hancock Bench

I love the simplicity of the Shaker original produced in the Hancock community, but I decided to experiment with that simple form by adding a graphic stolen from Van Gogh's "Starry Night."

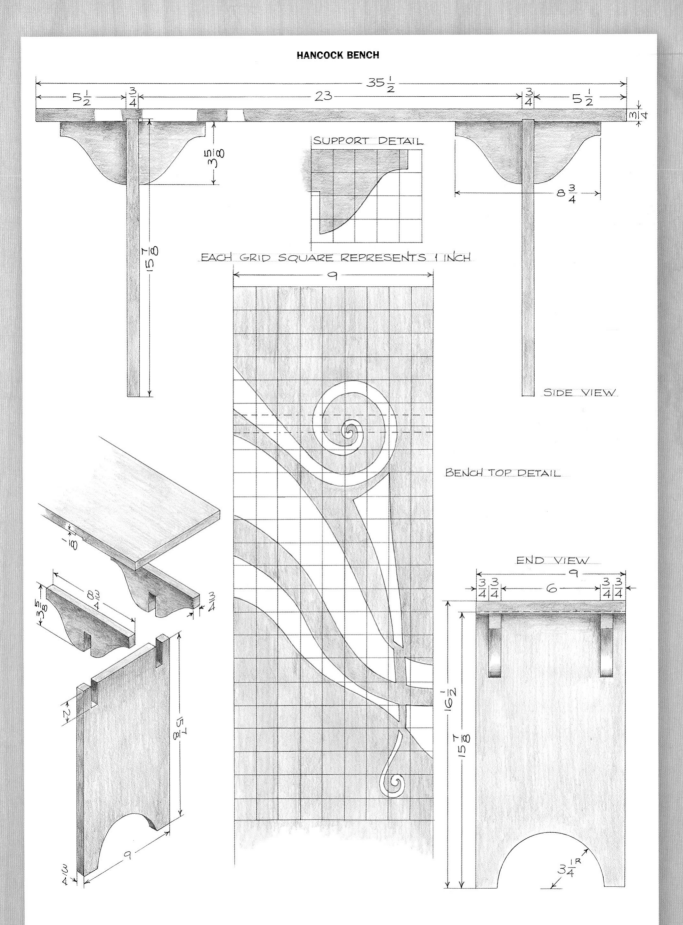

SUPPORT DETAIL

EACH GRID SQUARE REPRESENTS 1 INCH

SIDE VIEW

BENCH TOP DETAIL

END VIEW

$35\frac{1}{2}$

23

$5\frac{1}{2}$

$\frac{3}{4}$

$\frac{3}{4}$

$5\frac{1}{2}$

$\frac{3}{4}$

$3\frac{5}{8}$

$15\frac{7}{8}$

$8\frac{3}{4}$

9

9

$\frac{1}{8}$

$8\frac{3}{4}$

$\frac{3}{4}$

$3\frac{5}{8}$

2

$15\frac{7}{8}$

$\frac{3}{4}$

9

$\frac{3}{4}$ $\frac{3}{4}$

6

$\frac{3}{4}$ $\frac{3}{4}$

$16\frac{1}{2}$

$15\frac{7}{8}$

$3\frac{1}{4}$R

PHOTO 1 The bench is held together with wood screws, some of which pass up through the four support brackets into the bottom of the bench top. In this photo, I'm drilling the holes for those screws. Two holes must be drilled in the bracket at each location. One is the through hole — just large enough to accept the shank of the $1^1/4$" drywall screws I used in this location — the other is large enough to countersink the head of each screw. Remember that the countersink depth has to be set so that the screw tip will burrow as deeply as possible in the bench top without coming through.

PHOTO 2 The bench parts sanded and ready to assemble. Notice the plugs I'll be using to conceal the heads of the screws that pass down through the top and into the end-grain at the top of the two ends of the bench. Notice also the notches in those ends that will cross and lock with the notches cut in the brackets.

PHOTO 3 This photo shows how the crossed notches disappear in the finished bench.

PHOTO 4 The plugs covering the screw heads have been planed and sanded smooth.

PHOTO 5 If you want to give your bench a natural finish, this is the end of the road for you, but if you want to use a painted graphic (of any style), the next few steps will explain how that can be done. First, I sprayed on a coat of primer, working outdoors with a respirator.

PHOTO 6 I sanded away the raised grain with a piece of 220-grit paper and then sprayed several coats of white paint onto the primed surface of the bench top.

PHOTO 7 Next, I laid down a layer of painter's masking tape onto that portion of the bench top on which I was going to create a graphic.

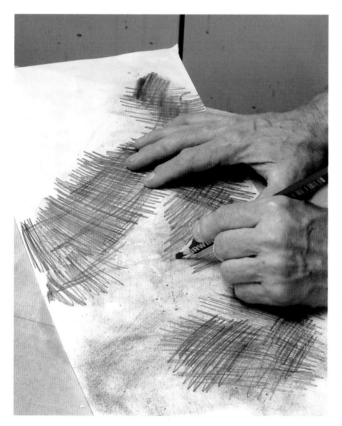

PHOTO 8 In the old days, before technology made it obsolete, people made copies of typed documents using carbon paper, which transferred typed impressions onto a second sheet of paper separated from the first by a sheet blackened on one side by carbon or a carbon substitute. Carbon paper was also handy for craftspeople wanting to transfer graphic details, and, while I'm sure there are now manufactured substitutes, when carbon paper disappeared, I got in the habit of making my own, by blackening, with a smear of pencil lead, the back side of a graphic I wanted to transfer.

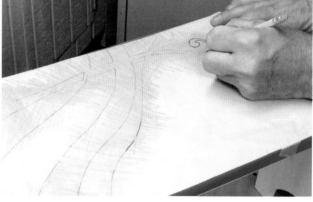

PHOTO 9 I taped, onto the bench top, the sheet on which I'd worked out the graphic. I then traced that graphic using firm pressure to ensure the pencil lead would transfer to the masking tape.

PHOTO 10 The next step is the most difficult. With an Exacto knife, I scored around the transferred design and pulled away the masking tape that surrounded the areas that would remain white on the finished surface. I then sprayed all the surfaces of the bench with several coats of deep blue and removed the masking tape from the white areas. The scoring left faint marks on the painted surface of the bench, but I chose to disregard them.

16

Windsor Chairmaking 101: Mike Herrel's New Take

Michael Herrel doesn't practice the art of Windsor chairmaking in a log cabin perched on an Appalachian hilltop. Instead, he builds his Windsors in the basement of a spacious home in the Columbus, Ohio, suburb of Bexley.

That's because Herrel was (and still is part-time) an investment advisor. But it's also because he has applied to this trade the same business skills and organizational expertise that have allowed him to succeed in the investment business. Yes, Michael Herrel is a successful craftsman, but he is also a successful businessman.

His showroom is the recently remodeled first-floor living room of the home he shares with his wife, Reeny. The room's white painted trim, hardwood floors and yellow walls provide a warm and cozy setting for the half-dozen handmade Windsor chairs and settees he displays there. A potential client viewing a chair in this carefully arranged environment can easily imagine how a Herrel Windsor would look in his or her own living room.

Herrel's home-based workspaces are thoughtfully arranged. His basement shop is immaculate. Machinery is neatly stowed in corners, hand tools are organized in drawers and clamps are hung in carefully spaced rows

Herrel believes that if you scratch anyone interested in woodworking, you will expose an interest in chair-making. "My contention is that every woodworker has wanted to make a chair, but when they look at it, it's beyond their comprehension." Herrel's mission, then, is demonstrate a simplified method of chair construction that can re-ignite dormant enthusiasm for craftwork in his students. "In my class," he explains, "I show all the secrets and tricks to make it a little easier."

behind his shaving horse. Bends and spindles are stored in neatly arranged cardboard cartons in the loft of the family garage. Herrel also stores turned legs in a freezer to retain the green-wood legs' moisture. He takes advantage of this moisture differential at assembly time.

A Break From the Investment Business

Herrel originally turned to woodworking as a way to take his mind away from the stresses of the investment business. Initially, his efforts followed a predictable course. He made Shaker oval boxes. He turned pens. He made a few pieces of furniture for his home. Then he met Joe Graham, a Windsor chairmaker who teaches from his shop east of Cleveland, Ohio. There, in Graham's shop, as Michael Herrel turned raw wood into chair parts, he found himself hooked.

"I've always wanted to make chairs, but it looked a little more complicated than casework, so I took a class. At first, I thought I would make one chair. But I fell in love with the process. You don't have the whine of the motors. You don't have the dust. It's almost like whittling. And you're always doing something a little different, whether it's turning or bending or spokeshaving." And most importantly, Herrel found that it got his mind "…totally off investments. I needed that," he adds.

He built one chair in Graham's workshop. Then he built another at home in his own shop. Then he filled his house with chairs. "I started to make some and give them away as presents. It got to the point where it was either stop making them or start selling them.

"At this point, my wife thought I was nuts. She said, 'Who is going to pay $700 for a chair?'"

That's when Herrel began to consider how he might market his chairs. His first stop was an art show in Worthington, another in Columbus, and he found immediate success there, selling six chairs in that first show. He then signed up for other shows, and purchased a trailer in which he could transport his wares from show to show. Then he began to consider teaching other craftsman the distinctive chairmaking method he had begun to develop.

As he looked for other venues at which he might sell his chairs, he researched the chairmaking field, seeking advice from some of the most successful names in the craft — Drew Langsner, David Wright, and Brian Boggs — all of whom shared ideas on building chairs, on marketing them

Herrel shaves a spindle in his immaculate basement shop.

and on teaching others to build them. Brian Boggs, according to Herrel, offered the most useful advice. It was Bogg's observation, for example, that chairmaking students were looking for information about how to build a chair, rather than how turn a leg or shave a spindle. This is an idea that informed the streamlined instruction process Herrel was devising.

Education Shorthand

The process of building a Windsor chair is traditionally taught in a five- or six-day class that begins with breaking bending stock out of a log and ends with the assembly of the various components. Within the scope of that five- or six-day class, students tackle the complex and physically demanding tasks of bending bows, shaving spindles, turning legs and excavating seats. It is grueling work even for an experienced chairmaker. According to Herrel, it's sometimes too much for the novice. "There are people midway through the process

that are exhausted and can't go on," he explains. Plus, he adds, there is so much information presented in that week that a student who goes home and wants to build a chair on his or her own can become lost.

Herrel's first abbreviation of the traditional format was created for the Woodcraft store in Hilliard, Ohio. In an effort to accommodate the week-end-only schedules preferred by many potential students, Herrel designed a curriculum spread across two, two-day weekends.

The next step was an even more radical contraction to a three-day class. To accommodate this format, Herrel began to provide students with parts on which some of the brute labor had been accomplished so they wouldn't need to spend two of the class's three days shaving spindles.

To simplify the shaving process, Herrel rough turned spindles to within an $1/8$" of their finished diameters. This allowed students to get a feel for the use of shaving tools without

Rough-turned spindles are stored in cartons in the loft of the family garage.

spending hours on the production of all the spindles required for a single chair. He also broke out and bent bows in advance, and, perhaps most important, he turned the baluster legs in advance. This part of the Windsor chairmaking process is one that confounds many novices and Herrel believes it interferes with a student's ability to evaluate his or her interest in the chairmaking process as a whole. "My objectives," he explains, "are number one, make it a fun class, number two, make sure everybody leaves with a completed chair and number three, make sure they learn enough to make a chair on their own."

In recent years, he has farmed out some of the parts preparation for his classes to other craftsmen, an idea he credits to Berea, Kentucky, chair-maker Brian Boggs: "He said," Herrel explains, "that you're paid to do finish work and the construction. Why not hire someone to get the material to where you can use your expertise?"

Because he often teaches in the relatively tiny classroom/shops of Woodcraft stores, Herrel's classes are

necessarily small, typically consisting of 4-6 students. His largest Woodcraft class was nine. Also because of small Woodcraft working spaces, Herrel has modified one of the most important and largest of a chair-maker's tools: the shaving horse. He got the idea from something he saw on a Web site called a shaving pony. This device

was made of 2×4s. Herrel experimented with the idea, ultimately designing his own shaving ponies made of much lighter aluminum and cedar. In fact, these are light enough that he can bring enough ponies for a Woodcraft class in his luggage on a plane.

Because of the success of his three-day Windsor classes in the Hilliard Woodcraft store, Herrel has been invited to teach at many other Woodcraft stores, too many for a single instructor to handle. Therefore, in the past couple of years, he has begun to train Woodcraft store owners or employees in the Herrel method of Windsor instruction so that they can teach the method in the 80 Woodcraft stores. He now has seven other instructors teaching his method at sites across the country and still needs instructors in California, Texas and New England.

The Woodworking Renaissance

Many of the students Herrel teaches are men and women about his age. They are often professionals who turn to woodworking because they remember the pleasures of high school shop

Herrel stores his green-wood legs in a freezer in order to retain their moisture so that he can take advantage of a moisture differential at assembly.

class. "I have had (as students) a chef, teacher, engineer, doctor — anybody who's interested in woodworking. As our generation ages, we're starting to retire. We now have the money and the time to do other activities. We think back to school, and we enjoyed shop, and I think that's why there's a renaissance in woodworking."

Herrel believes this renaissance has another 20 years or so to run until those baby boomers who remember taking shop in high school begin to lose the physical health required to work in the shop.

But he believes there is more at work here than simple nostalgia for high school shop class. He believes that men and women like himself, who have spent their careers in business, want to produce something tangible to leave behind after they're gone. "To have something that they produced. Something that their great grandchild can look at and say 'My great granddad made that.'" You're leaving a piece of yourself for future generations and there's something very comforting in that."

He is concerned, however, about the long-term future of craftwork

because, he notes, shop classes have been excised from many high school's curricula. "My kids never got any shop," he says. "They did technology. They got computer skills."

In the case of Herrel's two sons, this lack of high school shop class was mitigated by their exposure to a father who worked with his hands. In fact, both of Herrel's sons have taken his chairmaking class. "When they were little, I couldn't get them to do much woodworking, but now they both have taken one of my chairmaking classes. Both of them came up to me afterwards and said, 'I hate to admit this, but that was fun.'"

But in the larger world, in families lacking a parent with an interest in craftsmanship, there may be little incentive for children to explore this side of their natures.

Tallying Results

Herrel divides his workweek between investment work and chairmaking, with his work as an investment advisor accounting for perhaps 30 hours a week and his work as a chair-maker accounting for perhaps 35 hours. "In the morning, I play in my shop before

Bandsawn seat blanks are stored in his basement shop.

the markets open," he explains. "Then, if the day is slow, if not much is happening in the markets, I'll go down and work in the shop. Even after dinner, I'll work in the shop."

His 50-hour-week as a chairmaker is further broken down into two categories: hours spent preparing for and delivering instruction and hours spent making chairs. The balance between teaching chairmaking and doing chairmaking changes from year to year in response to fluctuations in the economy. "Last year my teaching just took off, but I wasn't selling as many chairs. This year, that's reversed itself. I'm not getting as many students, but I'm selling more chairs than I ever have." This, Herrel observes, points to an improving economy.

"This work helps me in my investments because I'm out in the marketplace and don't have to rely on the so-called experts to tell me what the economy's doing. If my high-end chairs are selling, that indicates that the economy is good. Last year my

These vanity plates announce Herrel's trade by making abbreviated reference to one of the more popular Windsor forms: the Sackback

Michael Herrel sizes spindle tenons with a Lie-Nieslen dowel plate.

chair sales were down but I noticed smaller types of artwork selling."

Although he didn't get into the field of chairmaking to make money, he has made enough working at this trade to put his two sons through college. In addition to the expected psychologically therapeutic benefits of working in a field dissimilar to investment advising, Herrel has experienced the joy of making, with his own hands, objects that will be passed down generation to generation, not only within his own family but within the families of those clients who purchased his chairs. Plus, his work as a woodworking educator has allowed him to share, with other craftsmen, the techniques he has developed for making Windsor chairs. Michael Herrel believes his tools and woodworking education were well worth the investment.

This unusual combination of office-chair base and Windsor seat and back has become one of Herrel's better-selling chairs.

Windsor Sack-Back Chair by Mike Herrel

PHOTO 1 Some parts of Windsor chairs need to be steam bent. In the case of the sack back I'm building in this chapter, the arm and the bow need to be bent.

Traditionally, chairmakers have preferred riven to sawn material because riven material — wood that has been reduced to a cross section of appropriate size by splitting — is seen as stronger because the grain runs continuously from end to end. However, as long as I keep the grain of the wood intact, sawn wood is fine for bending.

Just because the wood has been riven doesn't mean the grain of the wood is intact. In riving, the split will take the path of least resistance. If I don't have equal masses of material

on either side of the split, the split will go across the grain.

My steam setup consists of a five-gallon gas can filled with water which is heated to produce steam. I use a radiator hose to connect the

PHOTO 2 I center the wood in the bending frame and wedge it in place. Then I support the outside of the wood with my left hand as I complete the bend with my right hand. I place a dowel in the bending frame, then wedge the bent wood in place.

water can to the steam chamber, which is a length of six-inch pipe with end caps. I drill vent holes in the bottoms of both ends of the pipe to relieve pressure and in the center of the pipe, I insert dowels to support the wood.

Once I see the water is producing rolling steam, I insert the wood into the pipe and replace the end cap. I keep the wood in the pipe for forty-five minutes to one hour. I then have about two to three minutes after removing the wood from the steamer to complete the bend.

There are two sides of a bend, the compression side (inside of curve) and the tension side (outside of curve). I keep any grain that runs out the side of the wood on the compression side. Otherwise the wood will split as it is bent.

I keep the wood in the frame until the wood becomes loose in the frame, a process that takes several days. At that point, it's safe to remove the bend from the bending frame.

Using a band saw, I cut the oak for the spindles to $3/4$" × $3/4$", making sure to cut these pieces along the grain.

PHOTO 3 Spokeshaves come in all shapes and sizes which permit them to be used for different purposes. (Left to right: Lie-Nielsen - used for final finishing, Veritas - used for rough cutting; KCWCW Cigar - used for cutting inside curves, Harris - can be used for both rough cutting & final finishing, Antique - used for rough cutting, Home-made - used for rough cutting, Home-made - used for rough cutting, KCWCW - used for both rough cutting & final finishing.

Then I cut three spindles 25" long, two spindles 24", two spindles 23" and four spindles 12".

My shaving pony is the contraption I have in my bench vise in the photo below. The work is fixed in place through tension I apply by pressing on the shaving pony's foot pedal.

I set the spokeshave opening to about $1/32$". This thin mouth reduces the chance for the spokeshave catching on the grain of the wood and causing a tear-out.

Before I rough-shape the spindles, I draw a $1/2$" square on their bottoms, as well as a mark 5" up from the bottom.

PHOTO 4 In a perfect world, every shop would have a shaving horse, which is a traditional chair-maker's work station that provides craftsmen with a way to hold stock while it's being worked with shaving tools. Unfortunately, not every shop has the space for these fairly large devices. I designed something I call a "shaving pony" that permits a craftsman to hold material being worked with shaving tools without taking up so much space. A measured drawing is on the opposite page

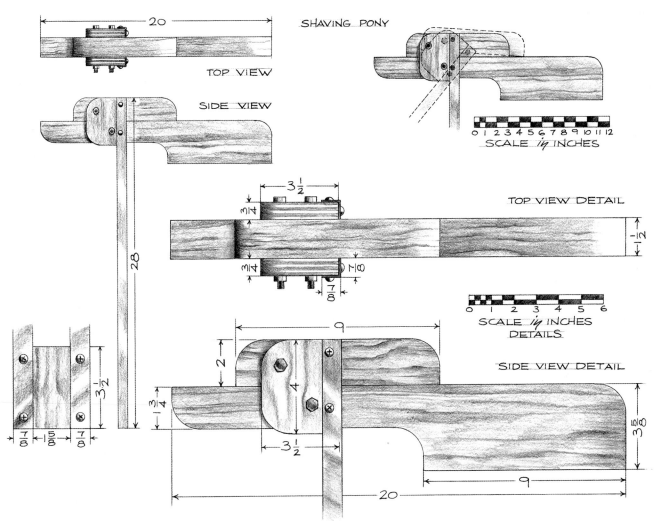

SHAVING PONY

TOP VIEW

SIDE VIEW

20

28

3 1/2

7/8   5/8   7/8

SCALE *in* INCHES

TOP VIEW DETAIL

3 1/2

3/4

3/4   7/8

7/8

1 1/2

SCALE *in* INCHES
DETAILS

SIDE VIEW DETAIL

9

2

1 3/4

4

3 1/2

3 5/8

20

9

PHOTO 5 I use a Lie-Nielsen Doweling Plate to create a $7/8$"-long tenon with a diameter of $1/2$". Be sure to size the bottom of the spindle before you reduce the diameter at the top of the spindle. You could break the spindle if you pounded the bottom through the doweling plate by hitting the small top of the spindle with your mallet.

I then use the Lie-Nielsen spokeshave to clean up the transition points. In fact, I finish the spindles with the Lie-Nielsen spokeshave, which produces a burnished finish that doesn't need sanding.

PHOTO 6 I use a washer with an inside diameter of $7/16$" to test for the correct measurement from the top to the 9" mark.

PHOTO 7 These are the tools I use for carving the seat. Left to right: a spokeshave, an inshave, an adze, a mallet, a curved gouge and a random-orbital sander.

PHOTO 8 The bench is an important tool that is often ignored. For my bench, I use a mini lathe stand with a 24" by 30" maple top that is 2" thick. I've mounted a vice with an adjustable face on the front and drilled several rows of $3/4$" holes for the holdfasts. This is a perfect bench for chairmakers.

With the spokeshave, I round the spindle to $3/4$" in diameter at the 5" mark, tapering to a diameter of $1/2$" at the bottom, inside the $1/2$" square I drew earlier. I use a Lie-Nielsen Doweling Plate to size the bottom of the spindle. I pound the spindle into the $1/2$"-diameter hole to make a $7/8$"-long tenon. Now I draw a $3/8$" square on the top of the spindles. I round the spindle to $3/8$" in diameter and rough-carve the tenon to at least 3" long. I use a Lie-Nielsen Doweling Plate to make the $3/8$"-diameter, 3"-long tenon at the top of the spindle. Next, I place a mark 9" up from the bottom of the spindle and

round the spindle from the 5" mark, tapering the diameter to the 9" mark, where the diameter will measure $7/16$". Last, round the rest of the spindle from the 9" mark, tapering to the $3/8$"-diameter by 3"-long tenon.

I use the same top and bottom dimensions for the short spindles that I used for the long spindles. The short spindles are rough-cut to $3/4$" × $3/4$" × 12". I draw a $1/2$" square on their bottoms, as well as a mark 5" up from the bottom. With the spokeshave, I round the spindle to $3/4$" in diameter at the 5" mark, tapering to a diameter of $1/2$" at the bottom, inside the $1/2$" square

I drew earlier. I use a Lie-Nielsen Doweling Plate to make the $1/2$"-diameter by $7/8$"-long tenon. Now I draw a $3/8$" square on the top of the spindles. I round the spindle to $3/8$" in diameter and rough-carve the tenon to at least 3" long. I use a Lie-Nielsen Doweling Plate to make the $3/8$"-diameter by 3"-long tenon. Finally, I round the rest of the spindle from the 5" mark, tapering to the $3/8$"-diameter by 3"-long tenon.

As it dries, wood shrinks mostly perpendicular to the growth rings (the layers of new wood added each year

(text continued on page 160)

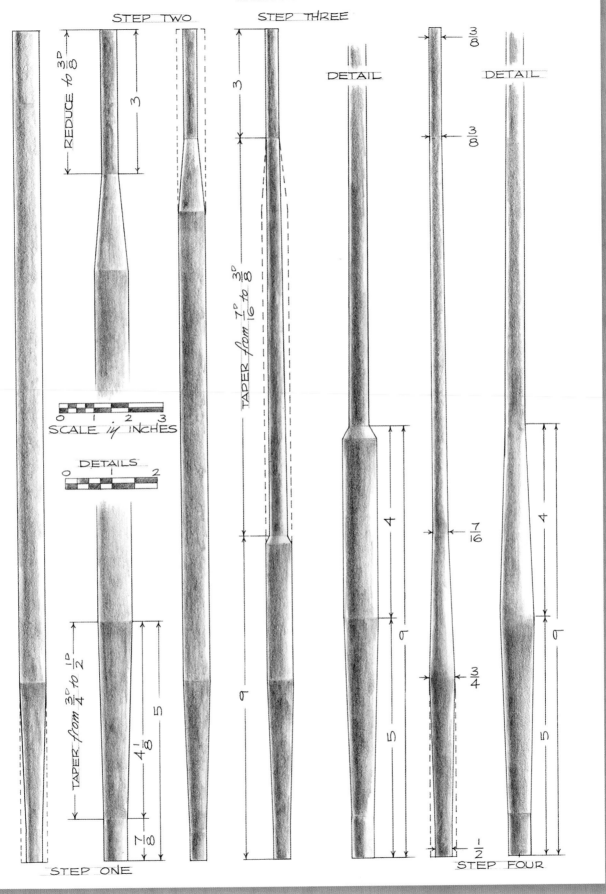

STEP TWO

STEP THREE

REDUCE to $\frac{3^D}{8}$

3

DETAIL

$\frac{3}{8}$

$\frac{3}{8}$

DETAIL

TAPER from $\frac{7^D}{16}$ to $\frac{3^D}{8}$

3

0   1   2   3
SCALE in INCHES

DETAILS
0   1   2

TAPER from $\frac{3^D}{4}$ to $\frac{1^D}{2}$

5

$4\frac{1}{8}$

$\frac{7}{8}$

9

4

$\frac{7}{16}$

9

5

$\frac{3}{4}$

4

9

$\frac{1}{2}$

5

STEP ONE

STEP FOUR

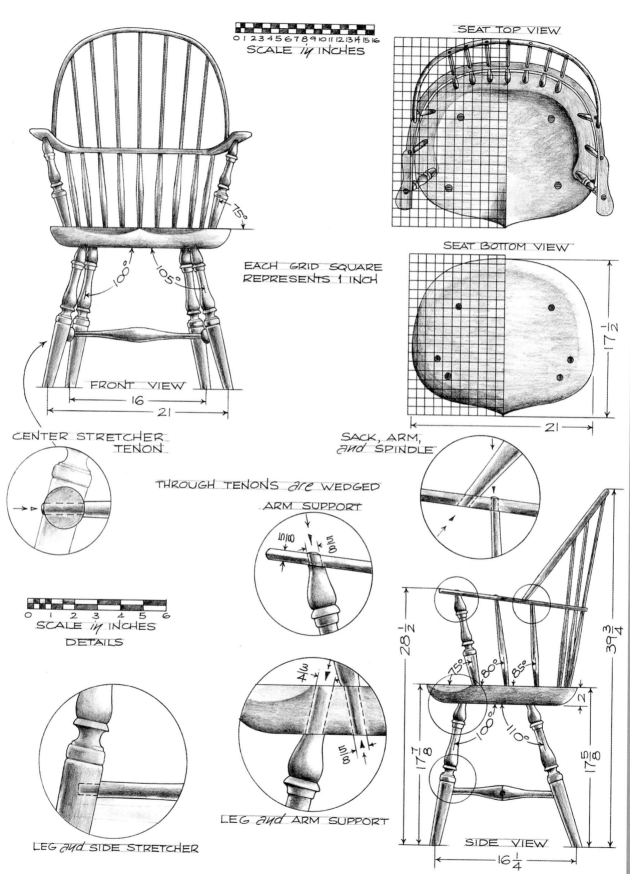

SCALE *in* INCHES

0 1 2 3 4 5 6 7 8 9 10 11 12 13 14 15 16

SEAT TOP VIEW

EACH GRID SQUARE
REPRESENTS 1 INCH

SEAT BOTTOM VIEW

75°

100° 105°

FRONT VIEW

16

21

17½

21

CENTER STRETCHER
TENON

SACK, ARM,
and SPINDLE

THROUGH TENONS *are* WEDGED

ARM SUPPORT

3/4

5/8

0 1 2 3 4 5 6

SCALE *in* INCHES

DETAILS

28½

75° 80° 85°

2

100° 110°

39¾

17⅞

17⅝

LEG *and* ARM SUPPORT

LEG *and* SIDE STRETCHER

SIDE VIEW

16¼

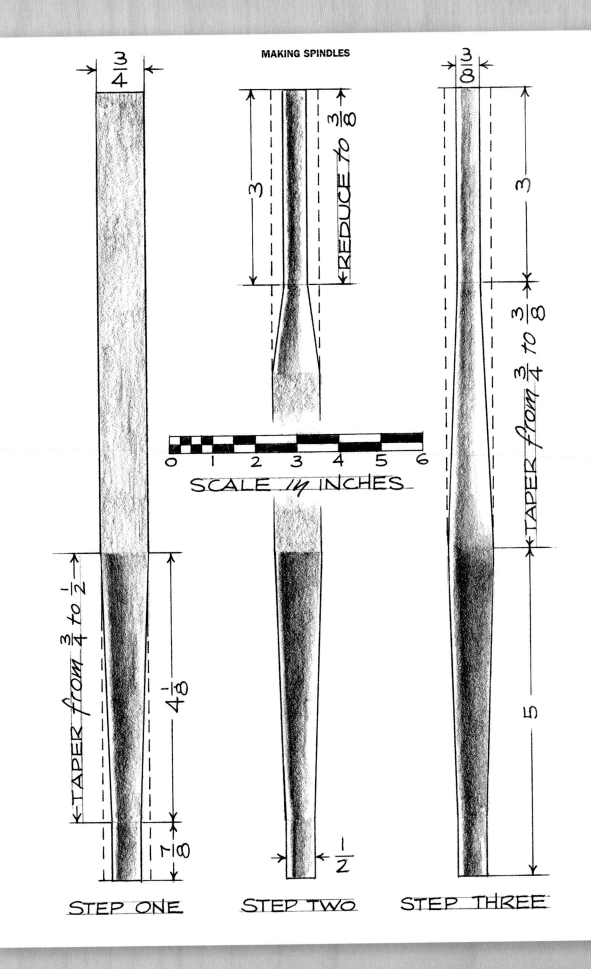

$\frac{3}{4}$

$\frac{3}{8}$

3

REDUCE to $\frac{3}{8}$

3

TAPER from $\frac{3}{4}$ to $\frac{1}{2}$

$4\frac{1}{8}$

TAPER from $\frac{3}{4}$ to $\frac{3}{8}$

5

0 1 2 3 4 5 6

SCALE IN INCHES

$\frac{7}{8}$

$\frac{1}{2}$

STEP ONE

STEP TWO

STEP THREE

PHOTO 9 I begin saddling (shaping) the seat, using an adze to remove the bulk of the waste, taking care to keep my blows well away from my feet. I first cut a trough down the center of the seat. By doing this, the successive cuts to the outer edges will chip out easily. This is not a precision tool, so I keep my blows at least an inch away from the gutter. I chop the lowest point, the back center, to about 1¹/₄" deep. The seat slopes from the front, almost in a straight line, to the lowest point.

PHOTO 10 I use holdfasts to secure the seat to the bench and then carve large chunks of wood from the seat with the mallet and curved gouge. I continue refining the edge around the gutter (the flat area at the back of the seat into which spindles and arm posts are later mortised) with the curved gouge. I begin smoothing the seat.

PHOTO 11 I use hand pressure to power the curved gouge across the grain to remove adze marks.

PHOTO 12 I then switch to an inshave to continue the smoothing process. I place the cutting edge of the inshave on the top edge of the gutter, then pull the inshave to the lowest part of the seat. By carving from the high point on the seat to the low point, I am cutting with the grain of the wood. This will give me the smoothest finish.

PHOTO 13 Once the seat is fairly smooth, it's ready to test for comfort. To make the test, I place the seat on a table about 18" above the ground and sit on it with my wallet removed. The seat should disappear beneath me. If I feel any pressure, I continue carving that area.

PHOTO 14 I use a random orbital sander to finish the smoothing process.

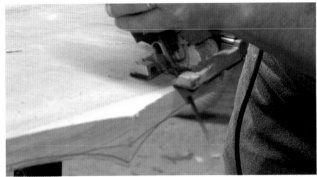

PHOTO 15 Now that the top of the seat is finished, I can start on the bottom. I need to round over the back of the seat bottom. Then spokeshave the front bottom to a knife's edge. This gives the seat a delicate look. I start by removing material from the bottom side of the front edge with a saber saw. I could use the spokeshave for this process but a saber saw (jigsaw) set at 45° removes the bulk of material faster.

PHOTO 16 I finish shaping the bottom with a spokeshave, following up with the random orbital sander. In order to work more aggressively by taking a thicker shaving, I need to open the mouth of the spokeshave to 1/16". Also, I make sure to cut with the grain to achieve a smooth surface.

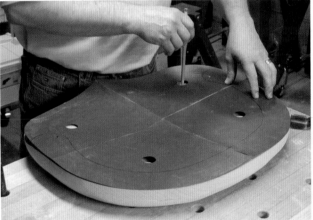

PHOTO 17 I use a template to mark where to drill the holes for the leg tenons.

LEG MORTISE JIG FOR CHAIR SEAT

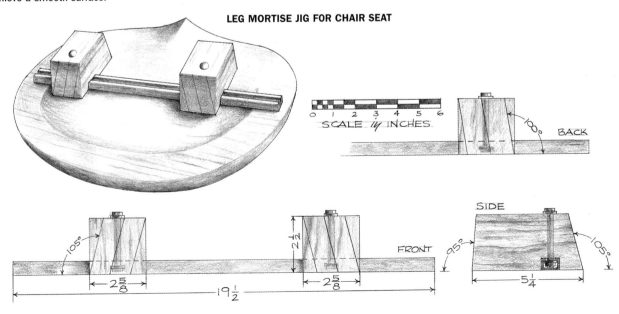

PHOTO 18 I attach the leg mortise jig to the seat, spacing the jig equidistant from the front and back marks and use an extension on the bit to help in the alignment.

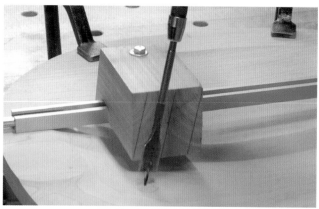

PHOTO 19 I align the $3/4$" drill bit parallel to both the jig and the line. I start the cut by breaking the surface with a fast rotation and then slow the speed. Once the bit starts to break through the bottom, I speed up and reduce the pressure. This reduces the chance for chip out.

PHOTO 20 I use the bit with an extension to make it is easier to sight the alignment of the bit.

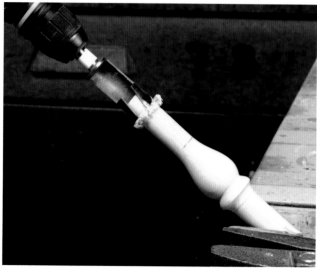

PHOTO 21 I create the leg tenon with a $3/4$" tenoning bit. Sometimes the mortise drilled by a $3/4$" spade bit is too large to fit the $3/4$" tenon made by a tenoning bit. In order to get the parts to fit properly, grind the spade bit to match the tenoning bit's diameter.

(text continued from page 154)

to the tree's circumference). I use this knowledge to build a stronger chair.

To insure proper orientation of the stretchers into the legs, I look for the grain of the wood in the leg. The grain moves from the top of the leg to the bottom. If I rotate the leg one quarter of a turn, I can see the grain make a circle on the turned leg. (I call this a growth ring circle.) This circle indicates the direction the stretchers will be inserted into the leg.

While keeping the body of the drill parallel with the bench top, I center the drill's axis of rotation on an imaginary line that connects the mortise locations on the two legs that will be connected with the stretcher you're installing.

Once I drill these mortises, I finish the bottom assembly. The mortises will immediately begin drying and the stretcher tenons won't fit after just a few hours.

Now I measure the distance between the holes (front to back) that

I just drilled into each leg. (I measure each pair of legs because these dimensions can be different. I want the stretcher to be a little long so it pushes the legs out slightly.) Mark the stretchers to length, then add $7/8$" to both ends of the stretcher for the tenons. Now I cut a $7/8$"-long tenon that is $5/8$" in diameter on each end of the stretchers.

I insert the side stretchers into the mortises in the legs and insert the leg tenons into the seat mortises, making sure that I align the side stretchers. To align the side stretchers, I rotate the side stretcher in the leg until the grain circles on the stretchers are facing each other. I place reference marks on the side stretchers and leg holes.

I clamp the center stretcher into position between the side stretchers for reference when drilling the mortise for the center stretcher tenons. I stop drilling when the tip of the bit breaks through the other side of the side stretcher to prevent tear-out. I complete the mortise from the center of the leg assembly while keeping the drill correctly aligned. Now I measure the center stretcher length. I want the stretcher to be a little long so it will slightly push the legs out. I mark the center stretcher to length, then add $2^{1}/_{4}$" to both sides of the stretcher for the tenons and mark. Next, I create a tenon on each end of the center stretcher. Each of these tenons measures $^{5}/_{8}$" in diameter and $2^{1}/_{4}$" in length. The tenons should fit loosely so I can tightly wedge them in later. If they are tight, I sand or file them until they fit more loosely.

I disassemble the parts and prepare to glue up the chair's undercarriage using Original Titebond. It's critical to remain organized throughout the gluing process. For that reason, I lay the legs and the stretcher for the right side of the chair on the right side of my bench and the legs and stretcher for the left side of the chair on the left side of the bench. This reduces the likelihood of making a mistake.

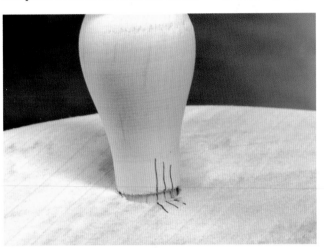

PHOTO 22   With the seat top-side down on a bench, I insert the legs into the seat. Make sure that the growth ring circles are facing each other front to back. I now pound them into the seat. I listen as I pound. The tone sounds more solid when it is in far enough. If I pound too much I can split the seat. Now place marks on both the seat and leg. These reference marks help when you reassemble the parts later.

PHOTO 23   I place a mark on each leg 1" above the top bead. I place the tip of the bit on one of the marks. By aligning the back of the drill with the mark on the back leg I will insure proper alignment. Then I center the bit, from side to side and drill a $^{5}/_{8}$"- diameter by 1"- deep hole into the legs for the side stretcher tenons. I place tape one inch from the end of the bit to let me know when I have drilled deep enough.

PHOTO 24   To use as a reference for drilling, I clamp the center stretcher into position on top of the side stretchers. I drill into the side stretcher and keep the drill bit parallel to the center stretcher.

I insert the glue into the leg mortises and spread it evenly. Excess glue will create hydrostatic pressure and prevent the tenons full insertion into the leg hole. I insert the side-stretcher tenons into the leg holes, making sure that I match the reference mark on the side stretcher to the reference mark on the leg that I made earlier.

Next, put glue into the side stretcher holes, insert the center stretcher tenons into the holes and make sure they are lined up correctly.

Finally, I spread glue in the seat mortises and insert the leg tenons into their mortises. As I pound the legs into the seat I listen. When the pounding tone sounds more solid, the legs are in far enough. (If I pound too much I can split the seat.) After everything has been assembled, take the time to wipe away all the excess glue.

Before I wedge the tenons on the center stretcher, I cut off the tenons so that each protrudes about 1/8" from the side stretcher. I will pare this extra length to form a decorative button after the tenon is wedged.

The wedges need to be aligned so that they are perpendicular to the grain of the part through which the wedged tenon passes. For example, the grain in the seat runs from side to side, so the wedges in the through tenons at the top of each leg must run front to back or 90° to this side-to-side grain direction.

I tap the wedges into place with a metal hammer. I listen for the sound of the pounding to change tones. Once it does, I stop.

To make the chair sit flat on the floor, I place the chair on my chairmaker's bench because I know it is perfectly flat. Then I use a wedge

PHOTO 25 I spread glue into the side stretcher mortises, insert the center stretcher into the side stretchers and set the assembly aside.

PHOTO 26 I trim the excess off the ends of tenons. The through tenons at the top of each leg and on each end of the center stretcher need to be wedged. I use walnut wedges because the color makes a good contrast with the maple chair parts.

PHOTO 27 To create space to start a wedge, I tap a chisel into the end-grain of the through tenon until an opening is created. While I tap on one end of the center stretcher, I support the other end with a wood block.

PHOTO 28 I chisel the leg tenons flush with the seat and use a chisel to create openings to start the wedges. Then I tap in the wedges, using a little glue to keep them in place.

PHOTO 29 The legs have all been turned with excess length. The next thing I do is cut them to a length that provides a comfortable seating posture and height.

PHOTO 30 I place three cut legs on the table and keep the long leg hanging off. Then I use a razor saw (not the backsaw) flush with the table to cut the fourth leg.

PHOTO 31 I draw a line from one side of the seat to the other, 6" behind the front point of the seat. Next, I measure 2" from each side of the seat and place a mark on the line I just made. This is the point where the arm post will be inserted into the seat. Now, I draw a curved line 1" from the back of the seat all along the gutter. A measured drawing is available on page 156.

to level the height of the chair from side to side, measure the height at the front of the chair and subtract this number from eighteen. This is the amount (in inches) that I cut from both the front legs. The marking gauge shown in photo 30 allows me to mark this cut in a way that will permit the bottom of the leg to meet the ground with a compound angle the way it should. I use a razor backsaw to make this cut along the lines.

I measure the height at the back of the chair and subtract this number from seventeen and a half. I use that number (in inches) and the marking gauge to draw a line around one leg and cut along the line. Finally, I place the three cut legs on the table and keep the long leg hanging off. I use a razor saw held flush with the bench top to cut the fourth leg to length.

The legs that I just cut have sharp edges that can easily be chipped. I use my spokeshave to chamfer the bottoms of these legs.

I round the protruding ends of the through tenons on the center stretcher with a paring chisel to create the decorative buttons.

I mark the back center spindle location on the one-inch line. (See photo 31.) Then I place three more marks on the 1" line, spaced 2" apart, on each side of the back center spindle location. These marks are for the remaining long spindles.

Finally, I place two more marks on the 1" line equidistant between the arm-post mark and the last of the long spindle marks.

I glue the tallest and straightest spindle into the center spindle hole.

PHOTO 32 I use an adjustable bevel set at 101° and place it on the gutter to drill for the back center spindle. Keeping the drill bit parallel to the upright leg of the bevel square, I drill the mortise 1"- deep and 1/2" in diameter. I use a bit extension to make it easier to sight and align the drill.

PHOTO 33 I glue scrap pieces of oak onto each side of the arm. Then I mark, cut and round over the grips.

PHOTO 34 I find the center of the arm by measuring equal distances from each tip of the arm grips and place a mark on either side of the arm. Any distance will do as long as the marks are equal. Then I place a mark equidistant between these marks and drill a 7/16" hole in the center of the arm.

By rotating the spindle before pounding it in, I can visually inspect the alignment. I want to be sure that this spindle is straight up and down when sighting it from the back of the chair. (It seems that all spindles have a slight curve)

The back of the arm will be positioned $8^{1}/_{2}$" above the seat. I need to clamp the front of the arm $9^{1}/_{2}$" above the seat. This holds the arm in place while I do the drilling. I can either make the jig using a 2×10 with cutouts for the clamps, or, as shown in photo 35, I can make the jig using T-tracks, wood and clamps.

I form a $^{3}/_{4}$"-diameter tenon 3"-long on the bottom of the arm post (my tenoning bit is only $2^{1}/_{4}$" long so I file and sand the bottom arm post tenon until it is the full 3" long) and a $^{5}/_{8}$"-diameter tenon $1^{1}/_{4}$"- long on the top

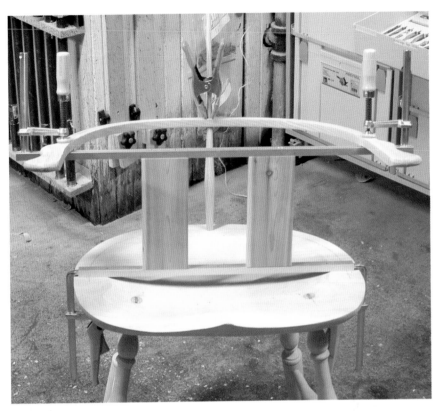

PHOTO 35 I draw a line from one side of the seat to the other, 8" behind the front point of the seat and clamp the arm jig to the seat on this line. I insert the center spindle into the armhole, center the arm on the jig and clamp the arm to the jig.

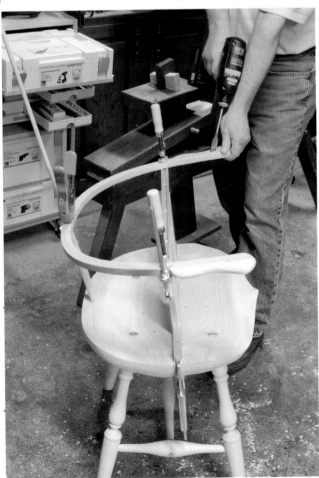

PHOTO 36 I drill a $^{5}/_{8}$" mortise 2" back from the front of the grip, ·aiming the bit at the mark for the arm post on the seat.

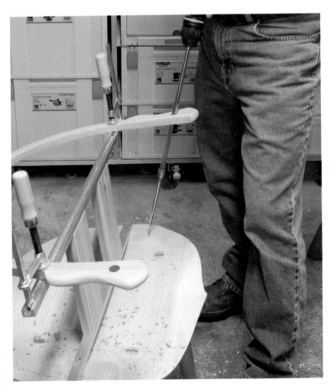

PHOTO 37 I can now insert the shank of a $^{3}/_{4}$" inch drill bit and extension through the $^{5}/_{8}$" mortise (chuck it up on the top side of the arm) and drill into the seat for the arm post. This gives me perfect alignment.

165

of the arm post. I want these top and bottom tenon joints to be loose. This helps prevent breakage during assembly. I file and sand the tenons until they easily fit into the mortises.

I cut the arm posts flush with the bottom of the seat, then wedge the tenon. Then I cut the wedge flush to the seat bottom.

For the long spindles, I mark the arm for three holes on either side of the center spindle hole, spacing them 2$\frac{1}{8}$" apart. For the two short front spindles, I place marks $\frac{1}{2}$" behind where the back of the grip intersects the bent arm. For the last two short spindles, I place marks halfway

PHOTO 38 I glue the bottom of the arm post into the seat and then dry fit the arm onto the center spindle and arm posts.

PHOTO 39 Now I drill a $\frac{1}{2}$"-diameter by 1"- deep mortise into the seat for each spindle. I use a bit extension and insert it through the armhole to get perfect alignment. Again, I use tape on the drill bit to let me know when to stop drilling. Also, I make sure that I drill the hole in the seat that corresponds with the hole in the arm.

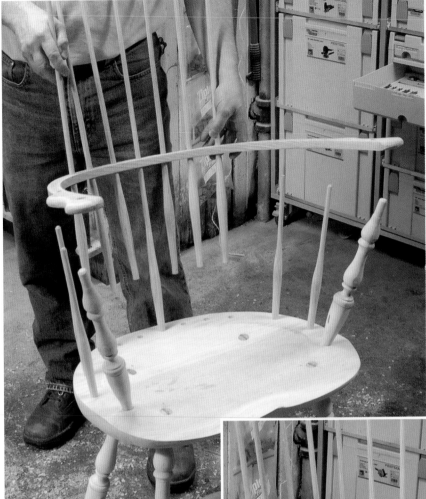

between the outside long spindle and the front short spindle.

I drill the spindle hole in the center of the arm, while aiming at the corresponding mark on the seat. I drill a $^3/_8$" hole for the short spindles and $^7/_{16}$" hole for the long spindle.

I remove the arm, finish sand the seat and arm, and then glue the short spindles into place in the seat.

I clamp the arm upside down in my vise. Then, I insert the long spindles into the proper holes. Next, I coat the short spindle, arm post and seat holes with glue. The long back spindles float and are not glued.

The back of the arm should be about $8^1/_2$" above the seat. Stand back, look at the arm and adjust the height on each spindle based on how the arm looks. Be gentle. Things can break at this point. If something doesn't fit, don't force it.

PHOTO 40 I flip the arm assembly over and insert the center spindle into the arm. Now, I insert all the tenons and spindles into the proper mortises in the seat and tap the spindles into their mortises.

PHOTO 41 Once the arm is assembled, I cut the arm post and the short spindle tenons so that $^1/_8$" of length protrudes above the arm. Then I insert and glue the wedges.

I place the wedge on the top of each arm post one-third of the way back from the front of the arm. I do this to prevent the arm from breaking out behind the arm post from the pressure the wedge creates. All other wedges are centered. Remember, the wedges are placed perpendicular to the arm's grain.

I button all the tenons that go through the arm.

PHOTO 42 I make a mark on the center spindle 13" above the arm. This is where I want the bow to intersect the center spindle. I clamp the bow between the short spindles on each side of the arm. I stand back and look at the bow to make sure that it looks balanced. If not, I make adjustments and re-clamp. Then I mark the bow above and below the arm. This shows me the length and position of the bow's tenons.

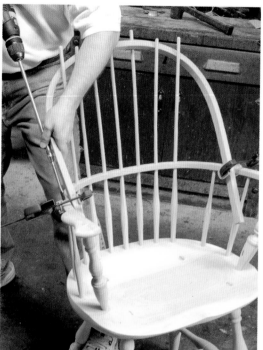

PHOTO 43 With the bow still clamped in place, I can drill a 3/8" mortise into the center of the arm and midway between the two short spindles behind the arm. I align the drill bit and extension with the bow for the drilling. I position the center back spindle straight up and mark the intersection with the center of the bow. I place three marks on the bow on either side of the center spindle, 2 1/4" apart. I make sure that the outside spindles appear to be curving or fanning outwards. If they don't, I increase the distant between these marks.

PHOTO 44 I round over all the edges of the bow with a spokeshave as shown.

PHOTO 45 I size the bow tenons with my spokeshave and a 3/8" tenoning bit. Then I finish the transition with my Lie-Nielsen spokeshave.

Now I tenon both ends of the bow. I use a tenoning bit, without an opening, for the oak. If I use one with an opening, it will catch the grain of the wood and break. This bit isn't made to take off much wood. I size the wood close to the finished diameter before using the tenoning bit. Then I use a 3/8" twist bit to slightly ream the arm holes. I want a loose fit to help reduce the chance of breakage.

I position the center back spindle straight up and mark the intersection with the center of the bow. I place three marks on the bow on either side of the center spindle, 2 1/4" apart. I make sure that the outside spindles appear to be curving or fanning outwards. If they don't, I increase the distant between these marks.

After the holes have been drilled in the bow, I use a 3/8" twist bit to slightly ream and enlarge the bow and arm holes. I do this to compensate for any drilling discrepancies. I sand the bow and test the spindles to make sure

they easily fit. All this is done to help reduce the chance of breakage. Next, I place glue in all the holes in both the arm and bow and then assemble the bow. The bow is weakest at this point, so I am gentle during this part of assembly. I check the look of the bow and make sure it looks balanced. Now is the time to make any adjustments.

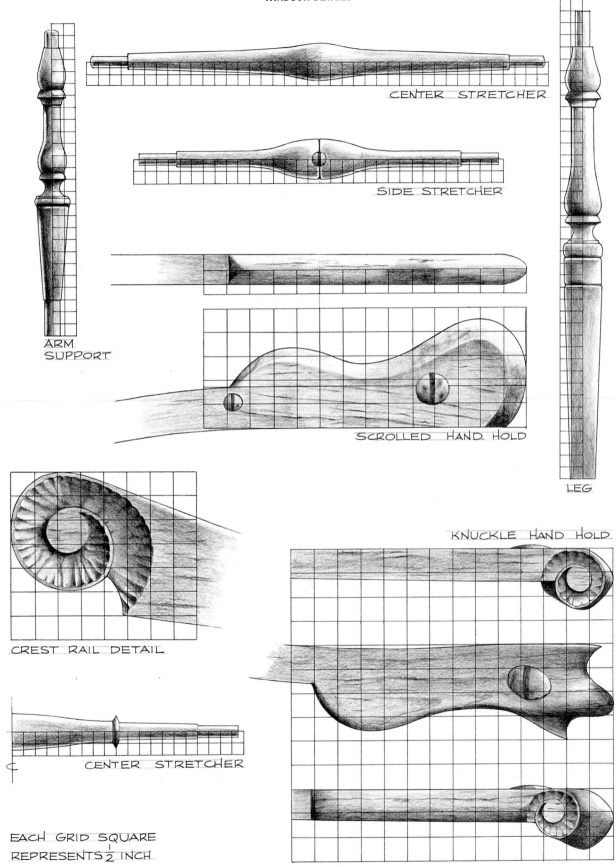

CENTER STRETCHER

SIDE STRETCHER

ARM
SUPPORT

SCROLLED HAND HOLD

LEG

CREST RAIL DETAIL

KNUCKLE HAND HOLD

CENTER STRETCHER

EACH GRID SQUARE
REPRESENTS $\frac{1}{2}$ INCH

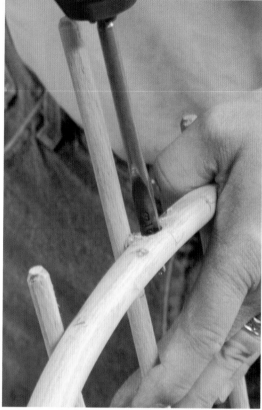

PHOTO 46 I test fit the bow into the arm. Once the bow looks good I cut the tenon off flush with the bottom of the arm. This helps me when I re-assemble the bow during gluing.

PHOTO 47 I drill at the marks into the center of mass of the bow, with the drill bit parallel to the spindles.

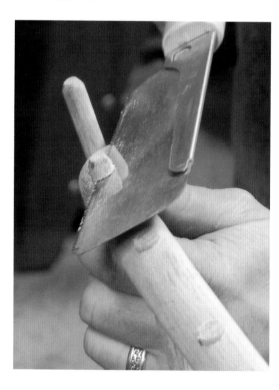

PHOTO 48 I cut the spindles $1/8$" above the bow, then wedge all the spindles. The two long outside spindles need to be wedged one third down from the top of those spindles. I do this to prevent the bow from breaking out below the spindle from the pressure the wedge creates. All other wedges are centered. Then, I wedge the bow tenons on the bottom of the arm and cut the wedges flush. Last, I button-shape all the spindles. Finally, I apply the finish.

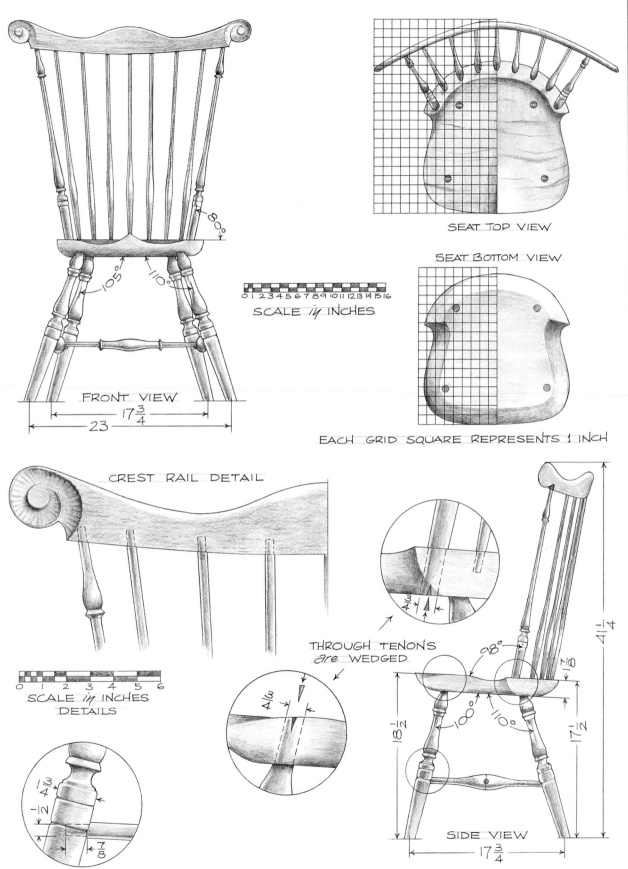

SEAT TOP VIEW

SEAT BOTTOM VIEW

80°

105°

110°

FRONT VIEW
$17\frac{3}{4}$
23

0 1 2 3 4 5 6 7 8 9 10 11 12 13 14 15 16
SCALE *in* INCHES

EACH GRID SQUARE REPRESENTS 1 INCH

CREST RAIL DETAIL

0 1 2 3 4 5 6
SCALE *in* INCHES
DETAILS

$\frac{3}{4}$
$\frac{1}{2}$
$\frac{7}{8}$

THROUGH TENONS
are WEDGED

$\frac{3}{4}$

$\frac{3}{4}$

98°

$\frac{7}{8}$

100°

110°

$18\frac{1}{2}$

$17\frac{1}{2}$

$41\frac{1}{4}$

SIDE VIEW
$17\frac{3}{4}$

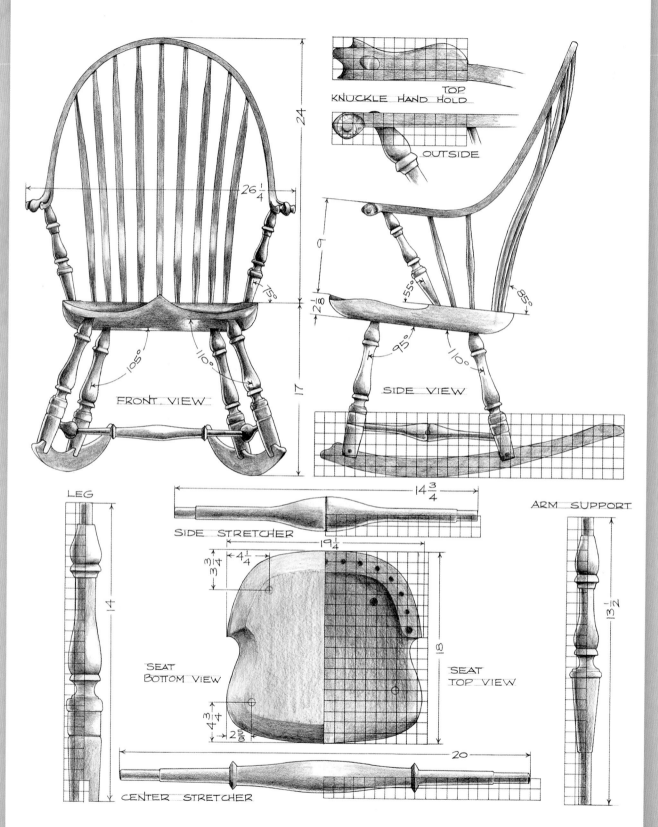

KNUCKLE HAND HOLD

TOP

OUTSIDE

FRONT VIEW

$26\frac{1}{4}$

24

17

75°

105°

110°

SIDE VIEW

9

$2\frac{1}{8}$

55°

85°

95°

110°

LEG

14

SIDE STRETCHER

$14\frac{3}{4}$

$19\frac{1}{4}$

$3\frac{3}{4}$

$4\frac{1}{4}$

SEAT
BOTTOM VIEW

SEAT
TOP VIEW

18

$4\frac{3}{4}$

$2\frac{5}{8}$

CENTER STRETCHER

20

ARM SUPPORT

$13\frac{1}{2}$

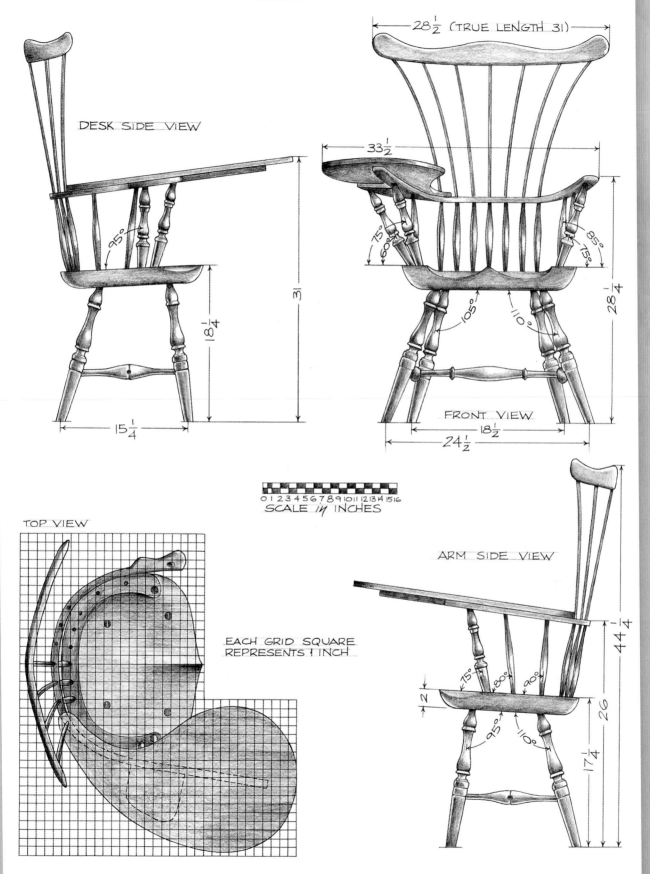

DESK SIDE VIEW

95°

31

18¼

15¼

28½ (TRUE LENGTH 31)

33½

75°
60°

85°
75°

105°

110°

28¼

FRONT VIEW

18½

24½

0 1 2 3 4 5 6 7 8 9 10 11 12 13 14 15 16
SCALE *in* INCHES

TOP VIEW

EACH GRID SQUARE
REPRESENTS 1 INCH

ARM SIDE VIEW

75°
80°
90°

95°
110°

2

44¼

26

17¼

Mark Soukup:
The Authentic Eye

Head south out of Gap Mills to the very bottom of West Virginia along a twisting, one-lane length of pavement to a valley bound on its eastern extreme by a bushy spine of hardwood-covered mountains, then turn left onto a narrow ribbon of gravel which passes between clusters of low trees and patches of grassy meadow. You'll come to the home and shop of Mark Soukup, a maker of Windsor chairs and period-inspired casework.

The valley is a winding, essentially treeless, expanse surrounded on all sides by hardwood forest. "East of us," Soukup explains, "there's more oak in that forest. Those sawmills over there are loaded with oak and poplar and pine. When you get into West Virginia, you get real good cherry and hard maple and other things like that."

The valley and the Soukup homestead are quiet. The nearest two-lane road is well out of earshot and doesn't carry much traffic anyway. On the left of the driveway's terminus is a garage and beyond that the Soukup's two-story home; on the right is Soukop's large shop. Beyond the shop is a fourth building, open on one side, in which stacks of neatly stickered lumber are drying. All the buildings are of frame construction and recent vintage and are well maintained.

This is an assortment of knuckled arms in mahogany, walnut and white oak.

It's the kind of peaceful, end-of-the-road place that seems just right for raising kids and just right also for building the meticulous period work for which Mark Soukup has become known.

The Influence of Herbert Edlin

Furniture makers aren't born. They're made, sometimes as a result of decades of sampling other careers, sometimes as a result of the encouragement of family and friends, and sometimes, too, a good book at the right time can be a powerfully directive force.

After graduating from high school, Mark Soukup left his childhood home in Cincinnati to attend Albion College in Albion, Michigan, in order to study ceramics like his older sister Ann, from whom he had acquired a taste for the pleasures of craftsmanship. He briefly operated a tree service in

Cincinnati, and, for a time, a lumber dealership in Washington State. When he first applied hand tools to wood, it was at the behest of his wife, also named Ann, who encouraged him to carve bowls and spoons. But ultimately, it was a book, *Woodland Crafts in Britain* by Herbert Edlin, that opened his eyes to the wide-ranging possibilities of woodcraft. Edlin was an English forester who wrote "… about traditional woodland crafts in Britain, and one of those crafts was Windsor chairmaking. This forester lived at a time when he could go out and mark timber for chair bodgers.* That really appealed to me," Soukup explains, "because it was a highly developed craft and yet involved very direct use of materials."

At the time he first encountered Edlin's book, Soukup and his wife were living in Washington State

where Soukup attended school and worked summers for a mountaineering school and the rest of the year as a small-scale timber dealer. During the late 1970s, the picturesque southern shores of Puget Sound were experiencing rapid development. This construction necessarily meant the removal of large numbers of trees, including some valuable hardwood species like Pacific dogwood and yew. "I would approach the developers when I knew there was timber in an area being developed. I would ask if I could get in there sooner." Soukup then cut the timber, had it milled, and dried it before selling the material to area craftsmen and boat builders.

The Soukups thought about buying property in Washington State, but land there was quite expensive. Plus, and more important, it was too far from their families back in Cincinnati.

*Chair bodgers were English craftsmen who set up rough shacks in the woods in which they lived while using spring-pole lathes to turn out large numbers of chair legs and stretchers which were then sold to chairmakers. Some bodgers claimed to be able to turn over 100 parts in a day. Jack Hill's *Country Chair Making*, still in print, published by David and Charles, contains photos of English bodgers at work. Edlin's book, unfortunately, is no longer in print. KP

Another Craft: Sheep Shearing

The Soukups settled comfortably into this new location, starting a family, joining a Mennonite congregation, and, while Ann home-schooled the children, Mark put to use the woodworking tools he had begun to assemble doing construction work when they lived in the Pacific Northwest.

The forested hills of the Greenbrier Valley in southern West Virginia are blessedly free of underground wealth. There's no gas or oil to tap with clattering erections of steel. There's no coal to expose by dozing away trees, grasses and soil. Plus, the hilly terrain is antithetical to the kinds of super-farms that in some Plain States locations taint the air and the ground water. The wealth of the Greenbrier region is vested in its forests and its traditional small-scale agriculture. It is, therefore, an environmentally stable region. Land there comes up for sale only rarely, and when it does, the price is often quite high because of its value as a setting for vacation homes and recreation. As a result, the Soukups lived in rented homes for 16 years while they scouted the area for a tract of land they could afford.

One of these rented properties was a 600-acre sheep farm which was home to about 100 ewes. This was a perfect situation for the Soukups because both had experience with sheep, and Mark had already established himself as a skillful shearer. After several years on this property, the Soukups developed a profit-sharing plan with the landowners that allowed them to rent the farm for a very modest amount while the Soukups worked the sheep. This allowed Soukup to supplement the income from his fledgling chairmaking business with income from the sheep operation. In addition, he began to travel across the country doing commercial sheep shearing.

In the spring, he sometimes sheared as many as 5,000 sheep, and during the rest of the year, he worked at his career as a chairmaker. "Within a couple of years, I was selling work (chairs)," Soukup explains. "Eventually we left there because the owners wanted to get rid of the sheep. We ended up renting another place for eight years or so."

At first glance, the processes of shearing sheep and working with wood might seem to have little in common, but they do connect — at least in Soukup's case. In addition to providing his family with a measure of financial security during the early years of his chairmaking business, sheep shearing exposed Soukup to the use of grit-impregnated rubber wheels which allowed tools to be simultaneously quickly ground and polished at temperatures low enough to eliminate the burning often caused by conventional wheels. He has taken this technique with him from the sheep barn to the woodshop.

Finally, in 1991, a 14-acre parcel of land went on the market at a price the Soukups could afford. The first building they erected was Soukup's shop in order to replace the tiny moveable building in which he had been working. The home, the garage and the drying shed, were put up as time and money allowed.

How to Learn a New Trade

Today, there are many places at which an American craftsman can learn chairmaking. Some are large multi-disciplinary schools like the Marc Adams School south of Indianapolis, Indiana. Others are smaller programs devoted solely to chairmaking like the Joe Graham school east of Cleveland, Ohio. But in the early 1980s, when Mark Soukup was learning to make Windsor chairs, there were no nationally known institutions offering instruction in the field.

Ann had once worked in a "Settlement School" in Kentucky, and they therefore felt a comfortable familiarity with the rural areas of the Appalachians, an area much closer to their Ohio roots than Washington State, so they began to look for a place in which to settle. A friend was able to lead them to someone who had a cabin in West Virginia, and the owner of the cabin offered it to the Soukups as their first residence in the state.

During the move east, in addition to their personal goods, Soukup carried with him the idea of using this new location as the setting in which he could continue to develop a craft he had recently begun to explore as a result of his exposure to Edlin's book: the craft of chairmaking.

This large, comb-back writing-arm-chair features figured walnut component.

Michael Dunbar's book, *Windsor Chairmaking*, and John Alexander's book, *Make a Chair from a Tree: An Introduction to Green woodworking*, both published in the late 1970s, were available. Both of these books provided Soukup with a theoretical context for the engineering of his early work. But, for the most part, Soukup, like many other craftsmen of the period who were investigating this field, had to teach himself. He learned by doing.

He later acquired aesthetic information from other published sources. For example, Charles Santore's *The Windsor Style in America* and Nancy Evans *American Windsor Furniture*. Certain issues of *The Magazine Antiques* were also helpful in this regard. But whenever possible, Soukup went to the source in order to study the design features of 18th-cen-

tury chairs, visiting both public and private Windsor collections.

After establishing himself as a chairmaker, Soukup began to add cabinetmaking to his repertoire of skills. At first, this happened almost accidentally. "As I looked for chair timbers, I started taking note of other things (timbers) that were available to me." He was helped in this new endeavor by the interest of his oldest son Robin, now 21, who expressed a desire to learn this new branch of woodworking.

"We home-schooled him through high school here. That was great for me. He eventually became skilled in a lot of things. I could put him to work doing dovetails and mortise-and-tenon joints." As a result of the availability of good material and the interest of his son, cabinetmaking became

a "… a logical thing. I was interested in doing it anyway." After all, Soukup explains, "When I make chairs, people want tables."

After working with his father for several years, Robin decided he wanted to go to school and he now works at a Mennonite mission in Poland, Ohio.

Good Material

Good material is hard to find for anyone working as a furniture maker. It is doubly hard for a maker of Windsor chairs because the kiln-dried stuff available at most hardwood dealers is simply not suited for chairmaking.

Whenever possible, Soukop buys logs and then has them custom-cut at a local mill.

There are three basic methods of sawing logs. By far, the most common is the flat-sawing method in which

Soukop's living room is also his showroom.

several boards are sawn from one face of the log until the cuts begin to approach the heart. The log is then rotated and sawn on an adjacent face. This is repeated until the heart — which is susceptible to splitting and twisting during drying — is boxed on all sides. The heart is then discarded or used for some secondary application. This is the method sawyers use most often because it's the method that produces the greatest number of usable boards from a given log. The second most common method is quarter sawing. There's more than one way to quarter-saw a log, but the intent is always the same: to produce the greatest number of boards having vertical grain, that is, grain running from the top face of the board to the bottom face. Because it is more wasteful of material and more labor intensive, it is the most expen-

sive method of sawing, but because it produces the most stable material, it is the method of sawing many craftsmen prefer. Soukup, however, prefers a third method: through-and-through sawing. This means the sawyer slices the whole log into boards the full width of the log. This produces a nice mix of quartersawn material (on either side of the heart) and flatsawn material (above and below the heart). It does, however, mean that the heart, sometimes called the pith, will be part of some of the boards Soukop harvests. This method also allows Soukup to maximize the number of wide boards (18"-21") each log will yield. This width is essential not only when sawing 8/4 poplar for chair seats but also when he's sawing figured material for large-scale casework.

When he is having logs sawn to his specifications, Soukup takes pains

not to interrupt the working of the mill. "These are big operations with lots of men, so whenever I do this, just for courtesy, I study the log as it's going down the main chain and think about how I'm going to have it cut, so when I go in the saw booth, I can just say 4/4, 5/4, 8/4. I've done it for enough years that I know what their limitations are — their carriage and their saw and how quickly that log can go through."

Because all the material (with rare exceptions) that goes into his shop is air-dried, Soukup must plan his work to match the drying seasons. For example, he schedules his cabinetwork in late winter. After drying his cabinet materials outdoors, he will then bring it "…inside in early fall and monitor it, and by the time it's January, it's usually down below 9 percent." It's at this point that he

178

turns from chairmaking to cabinet-making.

Years ago, when he was building mostly Windsors, this scheduling was less complicated than it is today because he is now building more casework which requires more 9% material. "It's hard to get enough wood indoors," he explains.

To assist him with the drying schedules, Soukup recently purchased a moisture meter, but his years of experience in the shop have enabled him to make reasonably accurate estimations based on the temperature and humidity in the shop.

He buys kiln-dried material only when he's offered a deal too good to refuse (or when he needs a tropical species like mahogany). For example, the drawer fronts on one of the three highboys under construction on the day of my visit are made of kiln-dried flame birch. Soukup explains: "One of the mills I buy from had 4,000 feet of birch, all kiln-dried, they had to get rid of. Actually, all I did was go through and pick out all the flame stuff."

Soukup recognizes the primacy of good material in the production of good work. "I'm a stickler for good timber so I always feel best if I can study the logs myself and get every bit of the log. Also, it is difficult to buy wide boards from lumber dealers. If you can buy them, they will be very expensive."

Selling Period Work

It's tough to make a living as a chairmaker even when you set up shop close to the urban centers which are home to many of the people with the means to buy good-quality handwork. But when you choose to live on the isolated rural underbelly of West Virginia, tough becomes, well, tougher. Most chairmakers in such a situation would take their work to urban shows in order to put it before the buying public. Since these shows often include Sundays on their

This square-back settee shows the design influence of Thomas Sheraton.

schedules, Soukup's Mennonite faith prevented him from taking part, so he needed to develop alternative marketing strategies.

"For a long time," Soukup explains, "I mostly sold through several high-end antique shops in northern and eastern Virginia. The reason I did that is because it was easy for me. I had five children and I didn't feel like being out hustling my work."

Although he has developed other marketing methods, Soukup continues to sell in a pair of Virginia antiques shops on a consignment basis, an arrangement that has always worked well for him. "All I have to do is have several sample chairs and a catalog. I've sold lots of sets of chairs that way. Normally, I work out consign-

ment relationships in which they (the shop owners) were taking only 15-20 percent, so I was able to price my work competitively."

Perhaps the most important venue through which Soukup sold his work was the now defunct *1740 House Antiques* in Virginia. His exposure there led to the most significant commission in his career: working for Monticello, the restored home of Thomas Jefferson in Central Virginia. Soukup's work can be seen at Monticello in the main entrance hall, the portico and elsewhere.

Soukup continues to sell through a gallery in Lewisburg, West Virginia, close to his home. Plus, he does two shows each year, one in Connecticut and another in Virginia.

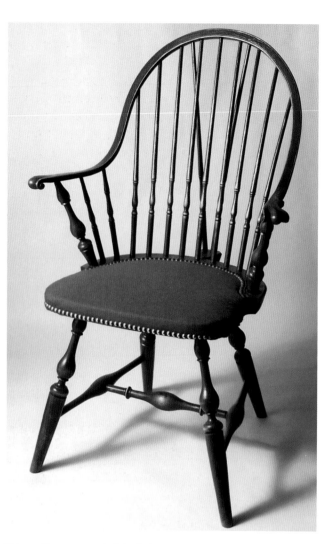

This continuous-arm chair is distinguished by an upholstered seat.

This large jointed-arm comb-back features mahogany arms.

He has advertised in *Antiques Digest* and *The Magazine Antiques*. Although he can identify few specific sales he made as a result of those ads, he does feel they have been useful. "I think it's important to periodically and consistently to get your name out there. They (magazine ads) can lead to contacts which are important in the long run."

But the key component in his current marketing strategy is his Web site. The site has provided Soukup with an opportunity to present to potential buyers the whole range of his work, as well as to explain how he goes about producing that work. While he has made sales directly off the Web site, without any additional contact at shows or galleries,

he believes his Web presence is most useful as a followup to contacts made in other ways.

Mark Soukup makes his living building period-inspired furniture, so making sales is obviously important. But for Soukup, sales are about more than just income. When accompanied by comments from purchasers, they also provide a means of validating his work. "There were some people who sold for me who knew that, and they made sure that people (buyers) wrote me letters." This is important, he discovered, because "…when you work by yourself all the time, pretty soon all your work just looks like junk to you. It's important to get feedback."

Not All Windsors are Created Equal.

Some chairmakers simplify the classic 18th-century forms. For example, reducing the number and complexity of the elements in a turned leg. In some cases, those changes may be unintentional simplifications, resulting from incomplete knowledge of the Windsor tradition or from skills not as sophisticated as the skills of the 18th-century masters who built the original chairs. However, in other cases, the simplifications are deliberate, intended to streamline the chairmaking process in order to maximize profit for the shops and/or factories which build these chairs.

But for chairmakers who have taken the time to educate themselves about the 250-year tradition of their craft, there are other — better — reasons for deviating from the 18th-century originals. Sometimes alterations may be suggested by the maker's own aesthetic taste. For example, in the case of one of Soukup's favorite chairs—a writing-arm chair—he mixed painted surfaces (like the original) with natural finished surfaces. He also reduced the size of the paddle (which supports the writing desk) on that same chair. This allowed him to reduce the size of the chair's undercarriage, resulting in a more compact composition.

In fact, the same could be said of nearly every 18th- or 19th-century form used in modern American homes. This is the paradox that confronts every maker and every consumer of period work. We now have other, less expensive, pieces in which to sit, at which to write, in which to sleep. "We don't need these objects anymore," Soukup observes, but "they can speak to us with a degree of elegance."

Other deviations from the classic 18th-century forms are suggested by clients who—for instance—might wish to combine features from several chairs into a single example. In such a situation, Soukup advises these clients about what kinds of features can be safely combined from an engineering perspective as well as from an aesthetic perspective.

The engineering decisions are straightforward. A non-traditional combination of elements will either work or not work, but the aesthetic decisions are more difficult to make, and it is in this context that an educated craftsman is most valuable. Any deviation from specific 18th-century forms is — in the strictest sense — unfaithful to those forms, but an educated 21st-century maker like Mark Soukup can experiment with those forms, introduce changes, and, as long as those changes are executed with

refinement and skill, they will be as authentically Windsor as anything produced in the 18th century.

The Authentic Eye

When you look out the windows of Mark Soukup's shop, you see grassy pastures and thickly wooded hills. When you step outside and listen, you hear the quiet music of nature. Your intellect doesn't confuse the 21st century with the 18th, but emotionally the two eras are connected here in this place in a way that probably isn't possible in an urban setting.

Inside his shop, Soukup wrestles with the same issues that confronted the 18th-century makers whose work inspires his own. He's aided by an array of good quality 21st-century power tools to augment hand work, but in the end, the process is still the

same. Windsor chairmaking is a continuing series of decisions a craftsman must make each day at his bench. How wide and how deep should this cove be cut? How sharply should this scroll be defined? How can they best achieve sweeping lines to mark the intersections of a chair seat's planes?

The quality of the decisions a craftsman makes at their bench is proportional to the quality of the study that preceded them. How many books they did read? How many photographs were studied? How many period chairs were examined? And perhaps most important, how many hours were spend at their bench lost in the contemplation of their craft?

All this preparation is important. Windsor chairmaking comes down to the nuanced observations of the authentic eye.

Carving A Windsor Arm By Mark Soukup

PHOTO 1 Opening up the carving of the knuckle: A saw kerf (shown in photo 6) between each of the lobes facilitates the opening using a low-sweep gouge.

T he knuckled hand-hold in these photos has an outward-spiraling volute, similar to the way the volute on a violin head is executed. One of the more stylish volute types, it was more likely to be found on expensive cabinetmakers' chairs than on Windsors in the 18th century. Nevertheless, elegantly carved mahogany and walnut arms were sometimes employed in 18th century Windsor construction, resulting in a chair that was stylistically more competitive with cabinetmakers' chairs.

PHOTO 2 Shaping the nose of the center lobe: The wider, 7-sweep gouge defines the radius of the center lobe. Photo shows the gouge following grain direction on the outside of the lobe.

PHOTO 3 Hollowing the space between the knuckle lobes: A moderately small, 8-sweep gouge roughs-in the rounded hollow. Narrower 9- and 11-sweep gouges will deepen the hollow.

PHOTO 4 Blending the hills and valleys: Specially bent files (both second cut and bastard) are useful for blending these transitions. (Files are easily altered by heating to cherry red, bending to desired shape and then re-hardening.)

PHOTO 5 Smoothing file marks: Use a card scraper which has been ground to the appropriate radius.

PHOTO 6 Opening up the underside of the knuckle: The low-sweep gouge (No.2 or No.3) leaves the correct radius of curvature for the outer lobes. Note the saw kerf dividing the center and left lobes.

PHOTO 7 Defining the volute center: Begin by rotating the No.8 gouge to incise the perimeter of the volute center precisely. A V-tool can then be used outside this incision to open up the volute carving. After opening with the V-tool, the No.8 gouge is used to define the volute center all the way to its base.

PHOTO 8 Removing the waste and defining the ramp of spiral.

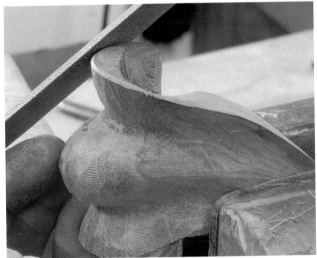

PHOTO 9 Breaking the edge of the lobe and volute transition with a file.

Glossary

Acorn finial: finial appearing in several variations at the top of many production chairs made at the New Lebanon Shaker chair shop

Adhesive: glue used to assemble wood parts

Adze, chair-makers: cutting tool similar to axe with gouge-shaped cutting edge set at a right angle to the handle

Ash: ring-porous wood with superior strength and bendability, lacks attractive color and figure, does not take stain well

Bandsaw: sawing machine equipped with a long flexible blade welded into a circle so that it can run continuously around the saw's large wheels

Bending: process of fitting wood plasticized by steaming (or soaking in water) into forms so that the wood will assume new shapes

Bending form: the wood forms into which plasticized wood is fit in order that the wood will assume new shapes (forms should impose an exaggerated bend in order to compensate for the inevitable spring back)

Calipers: tool used for establishing diameters on lathe turned work, consists of two pieces of metal joined on one end, often equipped with threaded rod so that diameter can be set and transferred from one turning to another

Card scraper: sheet of flexible steel, typically the approximate size of a 3 × 5 index card on which a burr of metal is rolled that can be used to lift shavings from grain too wild to plane

Carpenter's rule: a usually six-foot long rule with a hinge every 8" so that it can be folded and slipped into a pocket

Cherry: American hardwood prized for its color and figure, very photo-reactive, darkening over time, lacks the resistance to cross-grain fracture required of a premier chair-making wood

Compass: drafting tool used to scribe circles, consists of two legs one of which is equipped with pencil lead that rotates around the other leg which is fixed in place on a wood surface via a sharpened pin

Cushion rail: thin round rung-like turning running from the top of one back post to the other used as an attachment point for cushions Shakers offered to make slat-back chairs more comfortable

Doweling plate: Hardened metal plate across which are spaced holes in graduated size, a dowel or tenon can be reduced to an accurate diameter by forcing it through one of the plate's holes

Drawknife: any of a variety of knives equipped with a handle at either end, used to shave wood forms, typically used on softer green wood

Drill press: machine used to permit accurate drilling

Fingernail gouge: shallow-fluted turning gouge with the cutting end ground to a fingernail like shape when seen from above the flute

Finial: small decorative turning, typically appearing at the tops of back posts

Forstner bit: a drill bit capable of drilling a round hole. Used rather than a spade bit because it leaves a flat bottom in the hole and leaves cleaner edges.

Framing square: large square with two legs, the longer of which is 24" in length, used to check chair ladders for squareness at assembly

Front rung mortise jig (FRMJ): jig used to drill front (and back) rung mortises with consistent centerlines

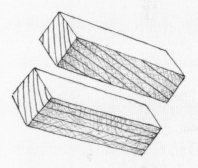

Grain runout: condition when the grain direction in a length of wood is not parallel with the sides of that length of wood, prone to fracture along the grain lines

Green wood: term used to denote undried lumber, used to identify any material not dried to a level appropriate for cabinet work

Gutter: a decorative groove paralleling the back edge of a Windsor chair seat

Hank: unit of measure for splint, approximately equal to one pound

Hickory: ring-porous wood with enormous strength, used for tool handles and chair-making, often found mixed oak and ash in the same chair

Inshave: two-handled drawknife with a cutting edge bent into a half circle, used by Windsor chair-makers to scoop out material from seat

Mallet: pounding tool used to drive chisels and gouges

Maple: a group of wood species of which "hard" maple is the best for chair-making as it combines strength with a density that allows it to support turned detail without crumbling

Mortise: an excavation in wood intended to receive a tenon

Mortise chisel: chisel thick in cross section to make it suitable for chopping mortises

Mt. Lebanon: the location of the primary Shaker chair operation, reached its zenith under the direction of Brother Robert Wagan

New Lebanon: an alternate name for Mt. Lebanon

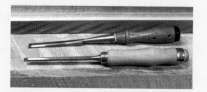

Paring chisel: chisel thin in cross section intended to clean up and square the sides of mortises

Pipe clamp: Clamp composed of a pipe on which is mounted a clamp head with a screw adjustment and a tail stock that can be slid to any point along the length of the pipe

Pommel: The finial at the top of the back post of a Shaker chair, also the top front section of a Windsor chair seat

Post: Name used by post-and-rung chair-makers to identify leg of chair

Rattan palm: A vine-like palm growing primarily in Southeast Asia with a hard outer shell from which chair caning material is made, the pithy material inside the hard shell is sliced to form rattan splint

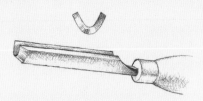

Roughing gouge: Heavy gouge formed to a "C" in cross section, used to transform square turning blanks into cylinders and for rough shaping as well

Rung: Any of the slender turned (or shaved) parts that connect a chair's posts

Saddling: Shaping a Windsor seat which is achieved by working the blank with an adze, carving gouge, inshave, and other tools

Shaving horse: a low bench with splayed legs designed to hold stock while it is worked with shaving tools, used while sitting on bench with feet applying force to lever which pins work under horse head

Side rung mortise jig (SRMJ): A device used on a drill press to hold the front and back ladders of a chair so that the side rung mortises (which enter the posts at compound angles) can be accurately drilled

Skew: A wide flat turning chisel used to create shapes and also to plane shapes on the lathe

Snipe: Deeper unwanted cut left on end of board by planer or jointer

Spindle: Thin, shaved parts from which a Windsor chair back is composed

Spade bit: A flat drill bit with a lead point, used by many chairmakers to drill rung and stretcher mortises, cheaper and more aggressive than Forstner bits, less aggressive than twist bits

Splint (ash): Strips of thin wood used by chair-makers for seating post-and-rung chairs, produced by scoring barked ash logs which are then beaten until the strips can be peeled loose, rare and expensive seating material

Splint (rattan): Strips of seating material taken from the pithy center of the rattan palm, the hard outer surface of which produces caning, a serviceable and inexpensive substitute for the more traditional ash splint

Spokeshave: A shaving tool related to both the plane and the drawknife, like the drawknife spokeshave is used smooth irregular surfaces, like the plane the spokeshave has a mouth to limit chip thickness

Spring-pole lathe: traditional tool used for turning chair parts, cuts when operator's foot applies downward motion on treadle after which tension in bent pole causes lathe to reverse directions

Stretchers: Connecting elements in a chair's undercarriage, pushes legs apart which keeps parts together using tension

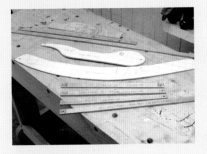

Template: pattern used to accurately place bandsawn contour or joinery without time-consuming measurement

Walnut: A highly prized American hardwood with a rich brown heartwood and light sapwood, despite beautiful color and figure not ideally suited for chair-making because of relative weakness

Warp: 1. Bend or twist from desired shape of board
2. those strands of a woven seat through which the weavers pass, typically those connecting front and back rungs

Weave: Those strands of a woven seat which pass through the warp usually in a well defined over/under pattern

Wedge: 1. Block of wood triangular in longitudinal cross section used to split logs into small enough sections for turning or shaving 2. chip of wood triangular in longitudinal cross section used to tighten through tenons and for decorative appeal

White oak: Ring porous wood of good strength and bendability, ideal for bent parts of Windsor chairs

suppliers

ADAMS WOOD PRODUCTS
423-587-2942
www.adamswoodproducts.com
Wood supply

CLASSIC DESIGNS BY MATTHEW BURAK
800-843-7405
www.tablelegs.com
Wood, wood parts

COLUMBIA FOREST PRODUCTS
www.columbiaforestproducts.com
Wood, hardware, tools, books

**CONSTANTINE'S WOOD CENTER
OF FLORIDA**
800-443-9667
www.constantines.com
Tools, woods, veneers, hardware

FRANK PAXTON LUMBER COMPANY
www.paxtonwood.com
Wood, hardware, tools, books

HIPURFORMER GLUE
800-347-5483
www.titebond.com
Wood, hardware, tools, books

THE HOME DEPOT
800-430-3376 (U.S.)
800-628-0525 (Canada)
www.homedepot.com
Woodworking tools, supplies and hardware

KLINGSPOR ABRASIVES INC.
800-645-5555
www.klingspor.com
Sandpaper of all kinds

LEE VALLEY TOOLS LTD.
800-871-8158 (U.S.)
800-267-8767 (Canada)
www.leevalley.com
Woodworking tools and hardware

LOWE'S COMPANIES, INC.
800-445-6937
www.lowes.com
Woodworking tools, supplies and hardware

ROCKLER WOODWORKING AND HARDWARE
800-279-4441
www.rockler.com
Woodworking tools, hardware and books

ROSEBURG FOREST PRODUCTS
800-245-1115
www.rfpco.com
Wood, hardware, tools, books

VAN DYKE'S RESTORER'S HARDWARE
800-787-3355
www.vandykes.com
Hardware and restoration supplies

WOODCRAFT SUPPLY LLC
800-225-1153
www.woodcraft.com
Woodworking hardware

WOODWORKER'S HARDWARE
800-383-0130
www.wwhardware.com
Woodworking hardware

WOODWORKER'S SUPPLY
800-645-9292
http://woodworker.com
*Woodworking tools and accessories,
finishing supplies, books and plans*

index

More great titles from Popular Woodworking!

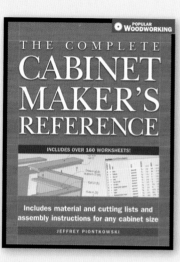
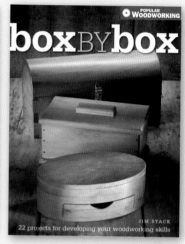
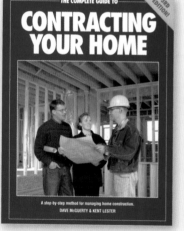
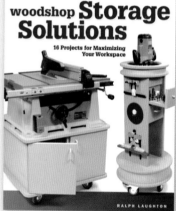